D1519892

1

<u>Acknowledgements</u>

Dedicated to the memory of Joyce.

And with thanks to all who have helped me to get this far. You know who you are.

Thanks too to my amazing editor, Heather.

I have no idea where I'm going
And no certainty how long it will take
Whether the path I will tread
Will go up, down or round
Is not something I plan in my head.

You may think I am lost
Stumbling round in the dark
But my assurance would say that I'm not.

I'm following the path I've chosen for me
The path that is flooded with light
So I follow this light
Not knowing where to
Believing I know what I need.

My desire for this path
Above other paths
May waver at times, I know
But I keep my eyes on
The love in the light
Take courage and firmly walk on.

Pat Suzie Tennent

Contents

5

Foreword, by Dr Sara Trevelyan

This is a remarkable book. It has been written not so much to take us into the dark spectre of the abysmal former life that Pat was unfortunate enough to have experienced, but to shine a light on how she found her own surprising way out of these horrors. To show that survival is possible. Also, to show how the psyche's own defence mechanisms, which are extraordinary if we have the willingness and humility to understand them, hold the key to living with experiences that would otherwise be overwhelming and potentially annihilating. There is only so much that can be endured...if we are taken beyond this threshold – what then? The recovery statistics from the kind of abuse described here are probably not encouraging were we ever to know them, but, in her own succinct words – recovery is hell, but it is possible.

Collectively, as a society, it seems that we have a much greater capacity as well as willingness to understand trauma than used to be the case. In recent times there has been a proliferation of accounts, written by courageous survivors, about abuse which help us to increase our understanding and our empathy. Those who have experienced the underbelly of life, who have had to endure severe violation and abuse, often have had to develop certain inner strengths and draw on the deeper resources which we all have within us. They find remarkably creative ways to survive these experiences. These accounts potentially show us the best of what we as humans are capable of, just as - if we dare to reflect on what these brave survivors have experienced - we can be outraged at those who cause such suffering. This is where compassion, deeper understanding, kindness and respect are all called for.

Pat's book hasn't been written for the purposes of exposing the horrifying abuse to which she was subjected from a young age. She does, however, present us with an outline of her early life. As an adopted child, the great tragedy of her life was that she had the misfortune to be brought up by a mother and grandmother who were both involved in a Satanic Ritual group. Through their unhelpful auspices she was exposed to the activities of this group throughout her formative years, only managing to escape from it in her late forties. What she had to endure as a consequence of this we might politely say "doesn't bear thinking about". Indeed, what she was forced to witness and was exposed to, in its most terrifying extremity, went way beyond the bounds of what her young consciousness could absorb. She was "saved" by a remarkable device of consciousness. This is that fragments of these experiences became split off into different "personalities", with the unbearable contents held and contained in separate compartments in her psyche. This resulted in Pat developing a condition which is sometimes known as Dissociative Identity Disorder, or, in more down to earth terms, Multiple Personality Disorder.

People with multiple personalities have been sensationalised in some of the earlier books and films which covered the subject. I remember reading 'Sybil' many years ago and finding this phenomenon of different personalities co-habiting in the one individual extraordinary, disturbing, mystifying, and quite weird. This sparked my curiosity for a while but I didn't take it any further. Since then, during years of psychotherapy training and ever deepening personal work, I have developed a much greater understanding of how each one of us has different aspects of our personality – sometimes called sub-personalities. Many of us have moments when we are aware of different competing parts in ourselves. Mostly, however, we are aware of these parts, and they are (to a degree) aware of each other. As one part of me sits writing this, another part would quite happily go and watch Wimbledon on the TV. Part of me (I think it's my inner child) has a sweet tooth and loves nothing more than to open a packet of biscuits. When I am doing my yoga practise notices that I'm gaining weight this part starts to behave more like a life coach and tells me that I should eliminate all the sugar items in my diet. I go into a room but forget what I've come to collect. I drive a long distance but can't remember most of the route. As Pat very helpfully points out, most of us recognise that we have different parts of ourselves which have contrasting preferences and opinions. This is a common experience in daily life. Lapses in memory happen embarrassingly often as I grow older - 'senior moments' seem to happen all too often!

The experience of complete inner fragmentation, though, isn't common. It tends to arise as a consequence of severe trauma - especially when this is experienced at a very young age. It is an extraordinary phenomenon, as I have learned in my practise over the years. It can also be disturbing. To observe someone changing appearance, voice and manner of speaking in front of my eyes is disorientating to say the least. I have had clients who have got lost on their way to see me – forgetting how to find their way to my therapy centre. When I have tried to tell them the way, they haven't been able (in a child state of consciousness) to read the street signs! Pat, however, has never been a client of mine, although there was a time early on when I could have anticipated this happening.

I met Pat in 2002 and we have journeyed together since that time in a way which has not always been easy to define or explain! I heard about her initially through a counsellor who was a supervisee of mine at the time. The existence of SRA – Satanic Ritual Abuse is highly controversial in some circles. I would have regarded it as off the scale in terms of my experience had I not been told about it 10 years previously by a close friend of mine who trained as a social worker in England, and who was involved at a national level for many years helping seriously abused children to communicate their traumatic memories and experiences. I helped her to write a book about her work called Sexual Abuse: The Child's Voice - Poppies on the Rubbish Heap. Her name was Madge Bray. She became my mentor and personal trainer in terms of understanding these experiences. Her insight had grown through listening to the voices of child survivors themselves. She extended her knowledge through conferences and through material which emerged initially from the

States. She provided insight into how these groups operated, and how their occult activities resulted in vulnerable children being exposed to unimaginable extremes of physical, sexual, emotional and indeed spiritual abuse.

As a therapist this was not an area I sought out or had a particular desire to work in. However, I have had a personal ethic in my counselling and psychotherapy practise over the years of not turning away anyone because of the nature of what they might have experienced. It is true that the stomach churning memories of some of those whom I have met and worked closely with have evoked physical responses of nausea in me, and I have felt stretched to the limit at times. In terms of my own capacity to absorb this extremity of experience, I have felt as though my mind has been stretched like chewing gum. How is it that these horrific and degrading activities continue to happen in an apparently unimpeded way in our 21st century world? Some people might dismiss them entirely, but as Pat points out, child sexual abuse - which we now recognise to be pervasive - was a taboo topic not so many years ago. The frontiers of what we can face and deal with as a society seem to move at a relatively slow pace because of our all too human sensitivities and fears. While this is understandable, it leaves those enmeshed in these hidden worlds profoundly isolated. If I didn't have a very well established personal discipline and strong faith, I couldn't have undertaken this work.

It is not surprising that there is still widespread denial about the existence of satanic ritual abuse. It is also not surprising that, as Pat describes graphically in this book, neither psychiatrists nor the NHS are especially well prepared to offer help to those recovering from exposure to these groups.

Her purposes in writing this book are not to describe these upsetting and (for most of us) incomprehensible forms of abuse, but to describe the process of recovery. She has spoken to me about this for years. I wasn't sure, due to the ongoing challenges which she was meeting in her life, whether she would ever manage to achieve this.

The news that she had managed to finish writing this account only reached me a short while ago. To say that it is a remarkable achievement wouldn't begin to describe how extraordinary it is that she has managed to give such a clear and well-articulated account of her process of recovery. As she says in her characteristically honest and forthright way, her healing is by no means complete. This doesn't mean that she isn't qualified to write this account. It qualifies her all the more, as what she has written describes what it is like to be still living as a survivor of such extreme abuse.

The gut wrenching truth is that those who have been exposed to excessive overwhelming trauma at any age, but most particularly when they are young and without adult protection, support or understanding to deal with what has happened, will take years to recover. Through being unable to express, release, integrate or heal the trauma, they will also acquire a whole range of symptoms, signs, and internal survival mechanisms which mean that everyday life is literally nerve wracking, and extremely difficult for them to manage. Pat describes this vividly and painfully. The human consequences are often isolation, hiding, shame, feeling like a complete failure in terms of the rest of the human race and extreme self-hatred resulting in repeated self-harm and more dangerously, suicide attempts.

When I was first introduced as a medical student to severely schizophrenic patients on the psychiatric ward I had a sense, even then, that it made much more sense to try to get to know them from the inside, rather than trying to understand them from the outside. They certainly had plenty of symptoms and some bizarre ways of expressing themselves, but I still had a sense of human connection with them. Fortunately, as a student I was left relatively free to roam the ward and I was able to meet some of these patients, not through their drug charts or through whatever DSM label had been put onto their condition, but in the way that I like to meet anyone who I encounter in my life - as individuals, and as people, rather than as patients. That they responded better when I approached them in this way isn't really surprising.

I left psychiatry relatively early on and subsequently in my life trained as a counsellor and psychotherapist in the person-centred tradition. I was attracted toward this because Carl Rogers, who was a renowned psychologist in America, built his whole approach on the basis of treating individuals with respect, believing that the all-important resources for healing were contained within them. The therapist's task was to be alongside and to help facilitate these resources to emerge. The medical profession's response at that time, which continues in many places, is based on a sometimes-spurious diagnosis, suppression and control – this all too often results in the patient being bombarded, sometimes relentlessly, with heavy regimes of psychotropic drugs. Pat describes this happening in her early years when she was subjected to the misplaced healing efforts of the NHS. Those who have florid, bizarre or disturbing psychiatric symptoms tend to be silenced, and reduced to zombies through the excessive use of strong suppressant drugs.

At the time when I met her, Pat didn't outwardly display any symptoms which would have caused her to look different from others who happened to be attending the daytime conference on SRA, which as she describes, was where we were first introduced to each other. She was of course much better qualified to speak about this difficult subject than most of us present that day. There were a few other survivors, but most of us participating were therapists or professionals. When Janet brought me across and introduced me to her it seemed that we could communicate quite naturally. Pat has a warm, easy smile. She looked slightly uncomfortable (not surprisingly!). She's a heavy smoker and probably reeked of tobacco. She was wearing denims and some kind of a top – standard type of dress for this kind of semi-professional/community type of event. She had attractive ginger coloured hair. She spoke quietly in a deep voice but showed a ready sense of humour, which she has maintained throughout – even through some of the most difficult times.

My initial involvement, as she has described, was to offer to give her some financial support towards her having therapy which in this instance was to be based around horse riding. I had set up a trust fund to assist those without the financial resources to access therapy which tends to be unaffordable for anyone living on benefits. I had to smile reading her account of her first visit to my therapy centre. She had expected me to interview her about the potential therapeutic benefits of horse riding. My own agenda was more along the lines of exploring how some involvement outside of where she was living with Janet and Derek might help her begin re-entering the world. It seemed to me that she was socially very isolated.

Things progressed from there. I continued to believe that what she really needed to do was to see a therapist, hopefully someone who had some experience and understanding of SRA, and who was accessible from where she was living at that time. As becomes perfectly obvious in Pat's account of this time – the last thing she wanted to do was to see another counsellor/ psychotherapist! She had a succession of unfortunate experiences in her twenties which at that time I was unaware of, of being "treated" by psychiatrists.

She had lost the relationship with the one counsellor, Janet, whom she had grown to trust, when Janet and her husband Derek ended up inviting her to share their home. This in my view was a courageous offer on their part, but of course it changed their relationship. It also raised issues of professional boundaries, and how they were planning for Pat to move on. This was where Janet and I eventually ended up falling out. Janet chose to end her relationship with me, and this felt appropriate once I became involved with Pat through offering her funding through my trust. I do know that despite raising these kind of difficult questions, had Janet and Derek not opened up their home and offered Pat of a place of safety, without any limit being set on the length of time she stayed, then we would not be reading this book and her story could have ended very differently. Leaving a satanic cult is a difficult and dangerous undertaking.

As Pat's account shows, the early years were incredibly hard. Eventually through the few outside contacts which she was able to make, her healing journey progressed in an unplanned and, in many respects, surprising way. The main contributors in the early stages were not trained mental health professionals. Her friend Mary remains a stalwart source of support and has become a lifelong friend. Joyce, the quietly spoken, utterly dedicated director of the retreat centre where I funded her first year of visits, proved to be her greatest ally on her healing journey. Joyce's work with Pat was of a spiritual nature, taking her into the deepest recesses of her being. This wouldn't have been possible if Pat hadn't been able to trust Joyce inside and out. The fragility and lifesaving importance of this basic quality of trust is something which stands out in Pat's account. She describes encounters with a whole variety of different health professionals who she encountered in her very challenging journey of healing – myself included! This is helpful and illuminating – even if occasionally uncomfortable. She holds up a mirror for those of us on the 'giving' end of the care which she received to be confronted with our own unintentional naivety as professionals. The quality which she ultimately received from Joyce which can't be quantified, measured, contrived or neatly packaged...is that of love. This is the most basic human quality which we all need, and hunger for, which can all too often feel impossibly out of reach for those on the periphery of society.

Having lost her own birth mother as a baby, Pat in a miraculous way, discovered someone who became her surrogate mother. Joyce is the true heroine of this account. Her capacity to offer Pat unconditional love and her deep faith were what ultimately paved the way to healing for Pat. Pat's story of finding and losing Joyce is at the heart of this book. Without Joyce it is doubtful that Pat would still be here and without Joyce this book would not have been written. As I believe that this account is one of great importance both for professionals as well as for those living with multiple personality (Ok, DID but I have never personally liked this term all that much!) we owe Joyce a debt of gratitude for seeing the light in Pat when others might have turned away. Many might have chosen to keep a personal distance in order not to have to confront her unpalatable background. While this response is understandable it would have further isolated Pat, condemning her to a continuing and difficult struggle living life in the shadows. May all those who live in this kind of set apart way, feeling their difference, crippled by their shame, hiding their past...also find in their own way this same medicine that Pat found through Joyce and others – the elixir of acceptance, trust and love.

Why does this simple medicine appear to work so well with an apparently complex condition? The reason for this is that as Pat explains, dissociation is a gift – without this capacity Pat and many others like her, would not have managed to survive and emerge from their traumatic past. As dissociation is a natural and indeed HEALTHY response to overwhelming trauma at a young age, it calls for our understanding and respect. Pat is encouraging others in her situation to empower themselves in relation to their therapy. When we are presented with the extraordinary capacity of the psyche to defend us from being overwhelmed, it is helpful to show a certain respect. It is not for us so called experts, for all of our training, to presume to know what is best for someone who has survived such adversity and who has found ways to manage the many and varied challenges of their lives. Partnering with them is what is called for. I am passionate about the importance of listening, and listening well, to those who have been at the sharp end of human experience. They have been where most of us would prefer never to have to go. The ones who have been there and who like Pat have survived, however precariously, have an important contribution to make to our understanding.

Ultimately our goal must be to arrive at a point where the kinds of degrading, and utterly destructive activities which exist in the sub human basement of our world and which Pat and unfortunately many others have been exposed to, need to be prevented and curtailed. We are a long way off from this at the present moment in time. I had hoped, after Pat suffered a repeated and frightening series of assaults, that the police might have been able to offer her protection, and even perhaps might have been able to apprehend the culprits. This was my deepest wish at the time. With the benefit of hindsight, I was naïve to believe that the protective auspices of the police would provide her with some measure of safety. One of the most difficult moments for me was when I realised that the rule of law which applies for people like me, did not extend to people like Pat. I have a basic sense of safety in this world because I trust that the police will act on my behalf if I need them. Unfortunately, this world contains many shadows and no profession is safe from them. The only solution to what was for many months/ years a continuing nightmare for Pat, was for her to move away, to the south of the country. The fact that she found her own way to do this, with very limited finance, is another of the miracles of her life.

There is so much in what Pat has written that deserves attention but perhaps the place to end is to re-assert her point that every individual with multiple personality (DID) is their own unique person. The message of Pat's life is that each survivor needs to trust their own healing process. If as the saying goes it takes a village to raise a child, perhaps we could say that it takes a cohort of professionals and non-professionals to help those emerging from the shadowy fringes of the world of abuse to reclaim their lives and step back into the light. Thank you, Pat, for showing us that this is possible. May your courage, and your wonderfully clear account of your own continuing process of healing, open the floodgates of possibility for all those others who are crying out for this. The final lesson which I take from this much needed book is that the key to recovery is love – nothing else can substitute for or replace it. Love is available and it is within us all in an abundant and limitless supply. If we truly understand that this is at the core, not just for Pat or Joyce, but for us all, miracles of healing are indeed possible.

Introduction

Before I tell you my story, I think it may be helpful to explain a bit about Dissociative Identity Disorder (DID). It's a complex condition which is poorly understood, and everyone experiences DID differently – so I'm afraid that I can't give you many hard and fast facts about the condition.

But I can assure you, from hard-wrung experience, that living with it is no picnic.

The condition was originally called Multiple Personality Disorder. In 1994 the name was changed to Dissociative Identity Disorder. Some articles state that the name was changed to reflect the fact that the disorder was not the result of many personalities, but rather a lack of a single 'integrated' identity.

The phenomenon known as 'Dissociation' is actually quite common. Everyone has probably experienced 'normal' dissociative episodes. For example, you may have fallen into a daydream while driving and afterwards been unable to remember how you reached your destination. Or you may have 'tuned out' of a conversation and missed a portion of what was said.

This 'autopilot' state, during which you lose track of yourself and your surroundings, is dissociation. Normal dissociative episodes tend to pass quickly. For people with DID, it's rather more complicated.

Let's move into the 'Identity' part of the acronym. This – the apparent existence of multiple personalities within one body – is the aspect of the condition which so ghoulishly intrigues the media. But it's not actually as bizarre as it sounds.

Again, our 'multiple personalities' are a born out of a perfectly normal phenomenon. Most of us have multi-faceted identities. There is no such thing as a totally integrated personality. This is a good thing - those with too inflexible an identity would find it hard to fulfil different roles or adapt to changing circumstances.

Having different aspects to our overall identities allows us to act differently in different situations. We use different aspects of our personality when (for example) being a mother, being at a business meeting, being a lover. The difference is, most people have an element of choice and control over how and when they bring out different aspects of their personalities.

This is not the case for someone with DID.

For people with dissociative conditions, these normal behaviours become extremely problematic. There is a sliding scale of dissociative disorders. DID is right at the top of that scale. Our identities are profoundly fractured, into many facets. The individual's ability to commandeer and control these many, many facets is limited to non-existent.

DID develops during the early years of childhood, often as a coping mechanism for repeated experiences of severe trauma. Tragically, this trauma usually takes the form of emotional, physical and sexual abuse.

Under the pressure of such appalling perpetual trauma, the mind fragments. It closes the emotions and memories associated with these overwhelming experiences away, into different compartments. This fragmentation is a sanity saving device, which allows the person to keep functioning at some level. By unconsciously transferring the trauma and related memories to other personalities it shuts the horrendous emotions away from the 'original' identity. When traumatic situations inevitably arise again, further splits occur, increasing the number of personalities who bear the brunt of the pain for the child.

'Splitting' is the action of a beleaguered but determined subconscious, willing to fight to survive. And, at the time, it works.

However, this psychic split does not go away when the trauma does. Ultimately, the abused child grows up with several different personalities and is usually unaware of their existence. These different personalities have suffered profound pain, and act in different ways from one another. Under certain triggers, these other versions may take over – causing switches in identity and behaviour which can be astonishing for the observer.

For someone to be diagnosed with DID they must have at least two or three different and separate personalities in the one body. These personalities (or alters/parts) are not actually different 'people', but parts of the single individual which are not functioning together as a whole.

I prefer to call my other inner people 'personalities' but everyone with DID has their own personal preference. Some refer to them as alters/inners/littles/parts.

Films and other media often portray people with DID as having evil personalities. In media representations, each personality is very distinct, and easily recognisable. In reality, people with DID do not necessarily 'switch' between personalities in such an obvious way.

The International Society for the Study of Trauma and Dissociation estimate that people can be in the mental health services for 5-12 years before a correct diagnosis is made. Patients can be diagnosed with several other conditions before the correct one is given. For example, many are diagnosed with Borderline Personality Disorder or psychotic disorders rather than with DID. The society further state that DID generally requires 5-10 years of therapy. Because of these complications, people with DID may get inappropriate treatment, or none at all.

There is no pharmacological cure for DID, but medication can help with the symptoms of PTSD (Post Traumatic Stress Disorder). Many people with DID have Complex Post Traumatic Stress Disorder.

There are currently no dedicated NHS services for Dissociative Disorders in the UK, and many psychiatrists within the NHS still refuse to accept that DID exists. There is no NICE (National Institute of Health and Clinical Excellence) guideline for the treatment of DID.

It is worth thinking about why NHS professionals find it hard to accept or diagnose the condition. I can only offer my own opinions, which are as follows:

Professionals have to see evidence of the existence of at least two separate personalities. This can be a problem as people with DID do not 'switch' on demand. In my case it has usually been my 29-year-old personality who has spoken to psychiatrists. Her role is to protect us, and she obviously feels we need protecting from psychiatrists.

Secondly, those with DID have usually suffered horrendous abuse from an early age. The abusers can be family members, or extended groups of abusers. I think professionals find this hard to believe.

And let's not forget that DID is portrayed in films and the media in a very dramatic and mostly inaccurate way. The general public's view of the condition is shaped by what they see, and professionals are part of the general public. A lot of stigma surrounds the condition, and even if a psychiatrist believes in the condition, they may fear that their reputation will suffer as a result if they admit to taking it seriously.

The best treatment guidelines are provided by the few centres which research DID. The International Society for the Study of Trauma and Dissociation gives a three-stage approach to treatment, which is as follows.

1) Creating safety and stability in the person's life. This includes grounding techniques.
2) Working with the traumatic memories. This can be very de-stabilising and needs to be done slowly.

3) The final stage can take years. This is the stage where integration of the personalities can take place and the person becomes a 'whole'. Though some people with DID prefer to just have good communication between the parts.

I have seven different personalities, each with their own name, characteristics and memories. We all have different ages, with the youngest one being 7 years old.

The result of this is a deeply fragmented life, with different personalities living parts of each day. We do not have good communication between us, and therefore have little or no recollection as a whole of what has happened while other personalities have been in charge - these gaps can last for minutes, hours, or even days.

Often, I can state different opinions in the course of one conversation, which is very confusing to whoever is listening to me. It is equally confusing for me. If I 'switch personality' when I am out, I get lost easily, not knowing where I am, or how I got there.

I hope that, during the course of the book, the reader will come to better understand the problems of trying to live on a daily basis with DID.

As for the extreme abuse I suffered, I have decided not to explain it in detail. There are many books already published which graphically describe the kinds of abuse people with DID have had to endure. Obviously, I give a few details but my reason for writing my story is to focus on the process of recovery.

Chapter 1

Life During The Early Cult Years

I was born over 60 years ago, in a small village in southern England. I was the only adopted child of an English father and Scottish mother.

My parents met when my father was training in Scotland to go and fight in the Second World War. Rumour has it that they met when my father was hanging onto a lamp post, so drunk that he could not find his way back to his barracks. That was the beginning of a romance which would see them marry at the end of the war and make their home in England, where my father had always lived.

However, when my father returned to his job as a gamekeeper, the romance began to falter. My city-born mother could not cope with the solitary life of a gamekeeper's wife, or with the guns that my father had in the house as part of his job. She convinced him to move to a small village, where he worked as a farm labourer, living in the lodge house at the gates to the landowner's 'big house'.

It seems, however, that she still did not settle to this new way of life. Only a few years ago I discovered that she frequently left my father and returned north for periods, only to return to him again.

Tragedy struck for my parents when my mother gave birth to a stillborn son and, to compound this bitter blow, was told there was no possibility of her being able to get pregnant again. After several attempts at adopting a baby they finally got me when I was 10 days old. Little was I to know that my own personal tragedy was about to unfold.

For seven years, my life was good. My early childhood was full of happy memories, both in terms of life on the farm and of being part of a large extended family. Strangely my memories from this time do not include my mother - although she was there.

I spent hours down on the farm with my Dad, either hanging out with him as he worked or playing with the children of other farm workers. This was, of course, in the days before health and safety which would certainly have forbidden the presence of children in work areas. At home, Dad had a small garden, and a few chickens. I loved helping him to plant things. During this happy time, my father gave me a love of gardening and the outdoors which would return to aid me, many years later, under very different circumstances.

Before I started school, Dad told me that I was adopted, in case I heard it from any of the other children. I did not really understand at that age, but he told me it meant I had been chosen by him and was special.

The village school had three classrooms, so each class had mixed ages in it. To read aloud to the teacher meant going to her desk, sitting on her knee and reading a bit to her. Doubtless sitting on a teacher's knee is another thing that would not be allowed today.

We sometimes went to Scotland to visit my Mother's family, and sometimes they came to visit us. For reasons I could not quite put my finger on, these were dark times, which began to cast a shadow over my life.

That shadow was soon to grow as one day a large van appeared, and our belongings were put into it. My cat, Sputnik (named after the first Russian sputnik to be launched) was set free into the woods, and my home was left behind. The lorry left and we got on a train north.

I have no memory of being told what was happening - but we were on our way to Scotland to live close to my Mother's family. Life was about to be turned upside down.

Life in Scotland was so very different in all sorts of ways. I was instantly confused by living in a tenement flat in a large city, where people spoke with an accent I could not understand. School was a large building with hundreds of pupils.

Being suddenly thrown into this alien concrete jungle caused me to withdraw into myself. I spoke very little, as my accent was made fun of. My refusal to communicate and not answer teachers' questions was seen as deliberate disobedience, and my years at primary school seemed to consist mostly of being sent outside the classroom to await the headmaster.

Eventually I made friends with another girl who, like me, had bright carrot orange hair. We became known as the terrible twins - though I am not convinced we ever did anything terrible. Rather, we were just different. My academic life was unremarkable and report cards always said 'could do better', 'does not apply herself', and 'seems to be in her own world'.

I guess if I was a little girl nowadays, teachers may look for reasons behind my behaviour, or question my home life, but in those days any strange behaviour was treated by the belt and not by questions.

Life at home was far from good. My grandmother lived downstairs from us, and I found out pretty quickly that she was a powerful woman whom no-one dared stand up to. My mother had wanted to return to be closer to her mother, but it seemed that her mother did not care for her. She certainly did not like my father and seemed to hate me.

The front door of her flat was always open and she spent lots of her time playing cards with friends. Each time I came home, I heard her tell them that, because my birth mother did not want me, I was obviously useless, would never amount to anything, and would never be part of her family. She proved this lack of belonging by never giving me birthday or Christmas presents, and always making a point of saying I was not worth buying for. She made me sit and watch my cousins opening their presents.

What I would never understand was why being adopted had suddenly become such a bad thing, and why my parents never questioned her or stood up to her. In my mother's eyes I could do no right and, because my father started drinking before he came home from work, I was on the receiving end of many beatings from him.

Perhaps I was the only one he could take his frustrations out on – the only one who would not fight back.

What I looked forward to each year was the two weeks we spent in England with my father's family. Years later I was to discover that his family were only polite to my Mother because they feared that if they were not she would put a stop to the holidays, and they would never see Dad and me again. As for me, I felt different in England, more whole and happy. But I was filled with a dread during the journey back north.

In Scotland, I always felt like a part of me was missing. Looking back, it is clear that a part of me really was missing, because the first split in my personality had occurred. Not only was I being emotionally and physically abused but during those primary school years, I was also being sexually abused by my grandmother.

The pain of this caused the first split. DID is often said to be a sanity saving device. When I could not take any more assaults on my being, my consciousness split, so that another personality took the pain and held the memories of the sexual abuse. Instead of just being me I became me and Suzie, each with our own individual characters and memories. We grew more different, though. While I have aged in years, Suzie has always stayed at age seven- the age I was when we moved to Scotland. I was not to know for years that different personalities held different memories, but it feels easier to write this from the position of knowledge that I now have.

During those years between age 7 and 11, Suzie was often alone with our grandmother. Initially being touched in her private parts, and then having objects inserted inside her. Often, Suzie was put in a dark cupboard where a box of insects was left to crawl over her. At other times, she would have her head held under water so she could not breathe. No wonder my mind split to cope with these assaults.

By the time I went to secondary school, I was becoming more and more withdrawn, often sitting staring out of the window, paying no attention. My mother did not encourage friendships - and certainly no-one was invited to our house. My interest in academic study was non-existent by this time, as I believed my grandmother's opinion that I was useless and would never amount to anything.

I became increasingly aware that I could not remember large chunks of the day but believed that everyone was like that. The truth of the matter was that the abuse was increasing - and so were the splits in my personality. 'I' became 'we', and my inner self came to consist of me, Suzie, Trish, Tracy, Heather (Suzie's twin), Cath and Ann.

Those early years of abuse by my grandmother were a grooming for what was to follow. She, along with others, was a part of a Satanic ritual abuse group which operated in the city.

The mention of ritual abuse tends to be met by disbelief. Personally, I think that this is because people cannot accept the horror of what happens in ritual abuse settings. Also, these groups are very good at being secretive, so proof is not easy to find. It is worth bearing in mind that generally people disbelieved stories from survivors of child sexual abuse when these first began to be spoken about. These days, it is an accepted fact that children can be and are abused by their parents or others. Horrific scandals like those involving Saville, or paedophile priests, have made us more willing to take seriously tales of abuse which would have been summarily dismissed as little as fifteen years ago.

Nonetheless, disbelief is still a common reaction when survivors of ritual abuse tell their stories. But why should they lie? The only people who feel the need to lie are the abusers. Most survivors speak of similar events, even though they have never met each other. There have been cases which have been taken to court and proved true (although these tend unfortunately to be the exception).

Abuse in a ritual setting is one of the worst forms of abuse, though all abuse is horrendous and extremely damaging.

Although in my case the involvement was generational, people with no family involvement can become involved simply because of choices they have made, or because they are vulnerable. What cults have in common is the use of power and a belief system which makes getting away very difficult but not impossible. Cults use hypnosis, mild altering drugs, extremes of torture and mind control to increase their hold over a person.

My personalities were taught that personal gain, indulgence and personal gratification were right, and that power was everything. The strong rule over the weak. Within the cult, the powerful have the right to impose their belief on others, and also to deny rights to others.

The perpetrators of these abuses tell people they can never escape, that no matter where they go they will be found, or that no-one will ever believe them. Most abuse has some measure of ritual involved such as grooming, secrecy, repetitive behaviours, organised groups of perpetrators (as in paedophile rings).

So why did I not tell anyone that I had been and was continuing to be abused? It seems a logical question, but the answer is somewhat complicated. I suppose one reason is that no-one asked. Even if they had, I could not have answered properly because so much of the information was held by other personalities and not by me. We had been told over and over not to tell because we would not be believed. Then there is the fact that my mother stopped me from having relationships and friends, so I had no-one to tell anyway. My grandmother told me that I was bad, and that I deserved what was happening. It seemed logical in my mind that, if the people closest to me were doing these things, then why would a stranger step in and stop it? My grandmother said I was bad, so I felt guilty. I did not want people to know I was bad, so I said nothing.

I began to live what became a double life. I finished school, leaving at age 16, and got a job - but all the time I was attending group meetings. I had no choice. Three of my personalities - me, Suzie and Trish - could function in a sense in the outside world, but the others functioned purely within the group. The fact that four personalities only existed within the group made it very easy for all of us to be controlled and to remain in that situation. At that point (and for many years onwards) I was unaware of the severity of what was happening. My other personalities were in a real sense protecting me from what was happening – although, having said that, I was not functioning very well.

Chapter 2

Abused Adult

Just before I was 17, instead of going to work one morning I packed a case and got on a train to London, convinced I had to get away. For the following 6/9 months I lived in a hostel for the homeless run by Catholic nuns in the East End. Even with no money or job I felt a sense of freedom and made the discovery that nuns have a fantastic sense of humour. Unfortunately, the Sister who was in charge of the hostel believed that I was in danger of ruining my life. She got in touch with my parents and escorted me onto a plane to return home. In actual fact I would have been in far less danger had I stayed in London.

I still remember nothing of the first three months after my return to Scotland. Any attempt to escape from the group is dealt with by extreme punishment, so I can only imagine what traumas occurred during that period. In fact, after my return from London I have no memory of my grandmother until the day she died several years later. I can remember some of my work life, but my home life during those years still remains a blank.

At the age of 18 I began training as a psychiatric nurse. I cannot remember how it happened, but by the age of 19 I had flipped to the 'other side' and become a psychiatric patient. I remember meeting a woman psychiatrist every Tuesday afternoon, during which time we said nothing for the hour- long session. She was obviously waiting for me to talk, and I was determined not to. Eventually, after several sessions, she said 'I give up'. The result was that I was sent to a psychiatric hospital in a different town. After three days I signed myself out and returned home. During the train journey I wondered why people were looking at me with a strange expression, only to discover at the end of the journey that my jacket still had the ward number and name of hospital on it.

Eventually, after a couple of years of job hopping I settled into a job as a ships' agent, where no 2 days were the same. At least work gave me satisfaction.

At this point, around my 21st birthday, my grandmother died. Her body lay in rest in her flat before the funeral, and each day I went into the flat to make sure she was actually dead and still in her coffin. At the funeral I was only there to make sure the coffin went into the cremator. Her death, however, did not put an end to my involvement in the group.

I married when I was 29, more by default than by choice. There was a man in my life whom I personally found to be boring, lacking in humour, and basically just not my type. His proposal was accepted by another of my personalities.

Many times, I called the whole thing off only to discover that it was back on again. Within 2 months of the wedding I became emotionally unwell and did not work again for many years.

My GP suggested I see a psychiatrist, but I did not want to after my experience at 19. I was quite shocked when my GP told me I had seen about half a dozen psychiatrists during my 20's. I had no recollection of meeting any of them, even though she tried to prompt my memory by reading excerpts of their reports, Whichever personality had seen these doctors had obviously not engaged with them at any deep level and seemed only to see them for a short time. Given that victims of abuse are told to tell no-one it is hardly surprising that none of us engaged with professionals.

It was around this time that a friend Sandra asked me if I knew someone called Suzie. After I told her that I did not she went on to explain what had been happening over several months. She said that when her young children came home from school I had a complete change of character, playing with her children and referring to myself as Suzie. I spoke as a seven-year-old and loved sitting on the sofa listening to children's stories. Initially I thought she was quite mad and could not grasp what she was saying. So, I did what I usually did when faced with the inexplicable. I ignored it.

However, at this point in life there were many things that did not make sense to me. I had been going to Church with Sandra and her family and, though I was interested in being there, all sorts of problems were happening during the service.

When a prayer was being said a voice in the back of my mind would alter the words of the prayer. Bible readings, would cause blasphemy in my mind and I found that my throat constricted so much I could not sing hymns; neither could I speak out loud the name of Jesus, no matter how much I tried.

The result of this was that my minister decided that I was probably demon possessed and sent Sandra and I off to see a minister who was experienced in such things. Though Sandra and I spent several hours with the minister I have no recollection of what happened. She told me later that the bruises on my arms and legs had been caused by the minister trying to restrain me, as I had been throwing the bible around, verbally blaspheming, and generally being violent. It was his opinion that I was the worst case of demon possession he had met. In reality what had happened was that he met a personality who was deeply into the group and found the mention of Jesus being superior seriously offensive.

Shortly after this, my minister went to see my GP to tell them that I was not mentally ill but involved in a battle between good and evil. As can be imagined, this theory did not go down too well with the medical profession. He was politely told to back off and leave it to them. They did, however, start asking questions about my memory gaps, and about what everyday life felt like.

I tried to explain how I often found clothes in my wardrobe that I had not bought, how I would find myself in places I had no recollection of going to, how I would 'forget' where my car was parked after having no recollection of going into town. How friends would tell me I had been out with them the night before but I was sure that I had spent the evening at home. I would hear that I had lost my temper with someone and not believe that I had even been there.

In 1985 I went to University to study for a degree at the same time as seeing numerous psychiatrists. I was on so many pills that one psychiatrist told me if he was on that many he would not be able to get out of bed in the morning. In 1986 I fell pregnant. I remember doing a home pregnancy test and suddenly feeling this huge panic when it turned positive. The strength of panic was terrifying, but later I came to understand that this was in fact a pregnancy that was the result of group abuse.

My GP decided that I was not well enough to cope with either a pregnancy or a baby so within five days I was in hospital, having a termination, and put on the pill to avoid a repetition. I was not at all happy about ending a life and was even more upset when my GP suggested I try to look at it in the same way as having a tooth removed and just forget about it. Even though I remained married until 1996, it was the termination which ended my marriage. On the other hand, as I do not remember marrying him, perhaps the marriage never really started!

By and large we lived separate lives, with him going to work early in the morning and heading to bed an hour after his return. When the doctors were discussing with him my need for a termination he sat and agreed with them but showed little actual interest or concern. On the evening before I was to go into hospital he calmly went off to bed, telling me to have a good day the following day. He neither took the day off, nor asked how I was when he returned home. Years later, when I said I wanted to separate, he told me I had never forgiven him for his attitude. Which was probably true.

In 1986, at age 33, I was finally diagnosed with DID. It was explained to me that there was no cure for this, but that the psychiatric services would deal with each individual crisis as it came along. I took this to mean that there was no medication to control it.

There then followed a cycle of psychiatrists, some of whom believed in DID, but most of whom did not. This resulted in me being put on large doses of medication usually prescribed to those who had schizophrenia. Each personality reacted differently to these drugs – so, while sometimes I could tolerate large doses, other personalities could not, and very often Suzie would be like a little zombie.

I have discovered over the years that Suzie is very important in the 'whole scheme of me'. Other personalities can be stressed or down, but Suzie is not affected. However, if Suzie is not happy, or is upset by something, our whole system picks up this unhappiness and is affected by it. This holds true even today.

In 1988 I completed my degree course and, after graduating, I went on to do a post graduate certificate and then a master's degree. My concentration levels were pretty poor and it was Trish (my 29-year-old personality) who did the studying and taking of exams. She was rather successful as it turned out. I do remember one professor asking why one of my exam papers had three different styles of handwriting on it.

After having being diagnosed twice with DID, around 1991 I was referred to a certain psychologist – a move which had unfortunate results. She was supposed to be an expert in DID, but within a couple of sessions she had decided that I had at least 17 personalities. She herself felt she was being followed on a daily basis by Satanists, and that they were dancing in her back garden on a regular basis in the middle of the night. As she lived in the middle of a row of terraced houses I began to conclude that she was crazier than her patient.

I saw her on an almost daily basis, got phone calls from her in the evenings, and was invited to her house. One morning after my husband went to work, two CID officers arrived, wanting to question me about where these cult meetings were held and who was involved. This psychologist was involved in teaching the police about ritual abuse and had taken it upon herself to send the police to see me. As I was not aware at this point about what happened at the cult meetings I could give no information. However, when they left three hours later, I realised that I did not know which, if any, of my personalities had spoken to them.

Things came to a head when I went to her office one day and she told me that she could not see me anymore as she had received a threat which warned that if she carried on seeing me then she and her children would die. This I took as further confirmation that she was slightly crazy herself.

About a year after I stopped seeing her, this psychologist was invited to leave the hospital after an incident with another patient. It seemed that she had been diagnosing numerous patients with DID. A report I later saw said that only one patient had been diagnosed with the condition prior to seeing her. As I got my diagnosis in 1988, I assume I was that one. I was asked by the hospital to give a statement of my experience with her, which I duly did. Apparently, her other patients were either in a distressed state or still saw her as a 'God' like therapist. For my part, I was seriously upset with her. I thought that she was emotionally unstable and was happy to help with the investigation of her. The hospital explained that they needed a patient's statement to go with theirs in order to report her to the British Psychological Society. What the result of this was, I was never told.

Many disbelievers of DID say that the condition is the result of an over enthusiastic doctor and a suggestible patient. In the case of that doctor, I can well believe that she used her patients to confirm her own delusion that Satanists were lurking around every corner. Somehow the False Memory people found out what was happening at the hospital with that psychologist and got in touch with me, offering to pay all my expenses if I took her to court for implanting false memories. I got as far as seeing a lawyer before deciding that I did not want to go down that road. I believed I had DID and felt that the False Memory people were in effect wanting to use me as an example for the media, in exchange for paying for legal costs.

At that point in my life, I was not prepared to accept what my personalities were telling me about the abuse. I coped in my usual way. I denied it all and tried to get on with life. I put the memories in a mental box, locked it, and threw away the key. Even though somewhere I knew the truth of what my personalities were saying, it was easier and less painful to 'blame the psychologist' - especially as I considered her more than a bit crazy.

During this time, I was still friendly with the Minister who originally thought I was demon possessed. By now he had accepted that I had DID. Shortly after my experience with the above psychologist, my husband came home with a copy of the local newspaper. The headline on the front page stated that a "Satanic Cult was operating in Town". The minister had gone to the press with the story, though thankfully my name was not mentioned. I rang him to ask just what the hell he thought he was doing, only to discover that the National Papers had already been in touch with him wanting more detail. Thankfully, after protests from me, he refused to be interviewed. If I was determined to go down the road of denial, I certainly did not want to find myself in the Sunday papers. Looking back, I wonder if I made the right choice. Perhaps things may have changed and justice would have been done. But, on the other hand, I was not ready to go public. Certainly, my other personalities were not ready, and they held most of the memories. I was pretty much still in the dark as to what was going on in my life. So, denial won the day.

I continued to see a community psychiatric nurse and a GP on a regular basis, but after the experience described above I was not in great emotional shape. I was waiting for referral to a psychotherapist and was convinced by my GP that - although he was experienced in DID - he was nothing like the previous one. When I did actually see him, we discussed at length what had happened during my time with the psychologist, and, although he was only around for two years, we agreed I could see him as and when I felt the need. This meant that there could be months between appointments.

In 1996, I separated from my husband. We sat on the kitchen floor agreeably deciding who would have what in terms of our belongings. I kept furniture I had taken into the marriage and he kept what he had. We were in fact very civilised about it, selling our house and dividing the money. My solicitor advised me that as the money had originally been mine I was being stupid by agreeing to a 50/50 split, but I just wanted out, and the separation agreement was drawn up as quickly as possible.

With my share of the money I bought a flat which was in very bad condition and proceeded to renovate it over the next couple of years. Unfortunately, it was in the same tenement building as my parents, so my mother was back in control of my comings and goings again. She had never been out of the picture, as I was expected to see her four times a week and she would pile huge burdens of guilt upon me if I could not make it for any reason.

Shortly after my separation, I mentioned to my father that I wanted to return to England. He asked me to promise not to go because, if anything happened to him, I would be needed to look after my mother. My mother's control over both of us was such that I agreed to stay. Life with the group continued as it always had. I attended meetings, with a number of my personalities becoming more and more involved.

Ritual abuse survivors are complex in that the control the group has over them extends to all parts of their lives. They are programmed to believe that telling anyone is useless because such incredible stories will not be believed. What I say later in the book seems to confirm this line of thought.

So, what did help me to finally talk? I guess it was a bit of lateral thinking by a GP. I had managed to hold down a job for three years in the mid 1990's but was still taking medication and self-harming my wrist. I ended up being signed off ill in 1998, and psychiatrist number 16 (or thereabouts) was looming on the horizon.

I am sure that said psychiatrist viewed the prospect with the same negativity that I did. My negativity towards psychiatrists had a simple explanation. As a child, no-one listened to me, treated me with respect, or allowed me to think I had any control over my life. In a strange way my dealings (or, more accurately, Trish's dealings) with psychiatrists had similarities. I had no control over the labels they gave me, or the medications. These 'experts' were not interested in what I thought. I did not feel valued or listened to as they sat taking notes, deciding on their own preferred diagnosis of me and latterly deciding that my remembered abuse and ongoing assaults were simply in my head.

My GP felt that yet another psychiatrist would probably not be productive. There was a Camphill Community in the area, and he suggested referring me to them. Camphill runs communities throughout the country and have houses where people with learning disabilities live and work. I went and saw the GP there and talked with him. They treat people as a whole being and not as a label using different therapies.

To be honest I found their approach refreshing (even though some of the therapies seemed strange to me). They practice something called Anthroposophical Medicine, and their approach is always to keep the focus on the individual and their capacity to change and develop health and wellbeing. This results in creating an individualised therapeutic programme.

Initially I began by doing curative eurythmy several times a week in one to one sessions with the therapist. It was one of the strangest therapies I have ever done and it took a while to realise that is was actually helping. For anyone who wants to know more about the Camphill approach it is easy to find on the internet. Eurythmy means 'beautiful rhythm' as the therapy is focused on bringing people back into balance, both internally and externally. It works with speech, gesture and music by bringing them into specially designed movements. Sounds and gestures are selected for the particular individual, and the goal is to evoke the body's forces which have been lost due to illness. Each session lasts for half an hour followed by a half hour quiet rest. Each vowel and consonant has a different movement and, though I have forgotten many of the particular movements I made, I still remember doing the sound and movement for 'B' over and over. I really must look it up some time and see why I did so many of them. On days when I did not feel like doing any of the movements, I also found it relaxing to watch the therapist doing certain movements, thinking that she could certainly do them in a more graceful way than I could.

After having done Eurythmy for several months I was introduced to the nurse and seeing her was built into my activities. We started with some massage on my lower back area. She explained that mental health problems do not just affect your head but the whole of your body, which to me made sense - though

32

being touched by someone was not something I found easy. I seemed always to be waiting for something painful to happen. After several sessions of the massage she asked what I would feel about having some oil baths. At first, I rejected that idea as a step too far. As the water had to be kept at a constant temperature, the nurse had to sit on the edge of the bath, ensuring the right temperature and adding the oils. I was not comfortable with this. However, after several conversations with her about it, I finally decided to give it a go. When I finally got past my embarrassment (or at least partially past it), I found that it was relaxing. At the end, she wrapped me in a large fluffy towel and I lay under a quilt on a bed so the oils could continue to do their work. That bit was seriously relaxing even though being wrapped in a towel was really unnerving. Talk about feeling vulnerable!

After that I did a bit of art therapy, but never really got the hang of that. Some days the therapist wanted me to use just one colour to make strokes across the paper until the whole sheet was covered. My patience (or rather lack thereof) failed to see the point of that. Then we started to look at different paintings. She would ask me what shape in the painting was initially drawing my eye to it, or what colour I was being drawn too. Unfortunately, I was more inclined to start making stories about the paintings. If there was a man on a path I would start wondering where he was going and what he was going to do. I don't think I was an art therapist's dream client.

While I was sitting in the waiting room for appointments I often saw a woman who came walking through or talked with the receptionists. She always said 'hi' to me, but somehow, I did not like the look of her. Probably because she was well dressed, well spoken, appeared confident, self-assured and thin. All the things I was not, which probably explained my feelings towards her. Mind you, I have always been pretty good at judging people before I even know them. One day I asked who she was only to find out she was the practice counsellor, Janet, so I was glad that I was not seeing her. However, it was only shortly after finding out who she was that the GP suggested I might like to do some talking therapy with her.

As I was relaxing into the various therapies I had been doing they felt that now I was ready to actually talk with someone. I only found out later that she was not too enthusiastic at the prospect of having me as a client because she had read the referral letter and thought that my DID may make things too complex. So, with neither of us being too enthusiastic, we began what was to be about two years of counselling. I remember telling her pretty early on in our sessions that if she told me I had more than three personalities, I would be out of there. I did not want a repeat of the psychologist who had decided on 17 within a couple of sessions.

Gradually, we built up a good therapeutic relationship in which I felt listened to and accepted. Trish also talked to her, as did Suzie. Lots of sessions were spent with me sitting on the floor talking, as somehow, I always feel more relaxed sitting on the floor. Or perhaps I just have a thing with professionals either sitting behind desks or positioning their chairs at what they think are perfect angles in which to encourage conversation. I liked her attitude of accepting that I had DID but not making a drama out of it. I have always steered clear of people who seem to get excited or intrigued by the fact that there is more than one of me. Over time some trust developed and 'we' took the risk of talking about the abuse. Not in a rush but very slowly, almost like 'we' were testing the water. Could she be trusted to believe what she was hearing, would 'we' be safe if we spoke? My mind was full of questions and fears. 'We' told her about our childhood and Trish told her that there were actually 7 of us and that four were still involved with the group. As some of the memories began to filter through to me, lots of things began to make sense to me. Unfortunately, it was a traumatic time. Hours were spent talking with the counsellor, more hours were spent in abusive situations, self-harming, and drinking to try to block out what I did not want to face. Groups of abusers do not like it in the least if they find out you have been talking with a counsellor over a long period of time and do everything they can to put a stop to it. It felt like things were reaching crisis point, and Trish decided it was time to get out of the group before things went badly wrong. She was the only one who talked with the other four personalities who were involved and got their agreement that they were willing to get away. So, the decision was made that before Easter of 2001 we would plan getting away to a place of safety. It was decided that I would go and live with Janet and Derek.

Unfortunately, it seems that the cult was all too aware of my plans. I don't know if one of my other personalities told them of the plan or if they just guessed. On the last evening of March, I discovered myself at a meeting of cult members. How long I had been there I have no idea. I was just aware that my whole body seriously hurt. What followed was some of the worst abuse imaginable, the details of which are still to vivid and painful for me to write about.

I rang Janet when I finally got home at about 2am. She told me to pack a case and move to hers. So, on the 1st April 2001 I walked away. Or, more accurately, drove away at great speed.

Chapter 3

The Process of Recovery

The previous chapters have been largely about the negative side of my experiences. Many books have been written which go into the details of abuse in quite some depth. When I started writing this several years I felt that I did not want to go into great detail, and I feel the same way now. I have outlined the story of my life because it is necessary in order for the reader to understand the context of my recovery. What I want to do from now on is to concentrate on the process of recovery - or, rather, the ongoing process of recovery.

To put the following chapters into some kind of time frame, I met some people who were hugely important in this phase of my recovery. In the previous chapter I explained how I came to know Janet. In 2002 I met Sara, and in 2004 met Joyce. Their influence on my life was such that I will devote a separate chapter to each of these remarkable ladies.

Anyway, back to April 2001, when I walked away from my life and moved in with Janet and her husband Derek.

Their actions in opening their home to me were unconventional to say the least, but as a result, I owe them a debt that can never be repaid. Doubtless many other professionals would see this as over stepping professional boundaries but had Janet not decided to provide me with a safe place, I would not now be in the position of writing this.

I should add that the GP at the medical practice where Janet worked knew what she was doing and supported it. In fact, he thought that the stability they were to provide was probably the most helpful thing for my mental health.

I continued to do some alternative therapies at the medical practice she worked at until September 2002. In the GP's discharge letter, he said that my two years of attendance there had brought consistent improvements in many aspects of my problems. He stated that the real breakthroughs had occurred since I had been living with Janet and Derek, in a supported setting with ongoing therapeutic activities. I think that, for me, the most important and therapeutic activity was gardening, which I will talk about in more detail later in the chapter. He felt that this protective environment was essential for me to maintain my current level of functioning and ability. I think that this letter was one of the few times a professional had something positive to say about me. But being treated as a person, rather than as a label, or as a symptom to be medicated, made all the difference to my willingness to engage.

Obviously, the day I moved in with them, Janet stopped being my counsellor and became a friend. In her words it was a pretty intense time. These changes to our relationship took us both time to adjust to. I think during the final months of our counselling relationship and the first year of living with her my mind was largely unaware of what was happening. Looking back on it I guess we handled the transition in the best way that we individually could.

Derek met me on the day I moved in. He is a truly amazing guy, who has a truly deep understanding of both the world and of people - not to mention a great sense of humour! It was the love and support I was given by these two very special people that allowed me to begin my healing, and to begin to learn to live in a world that was completely alien to me.

As they lived in 5 acres in the countryside I had the space, both physically and emotionally, in which to begin to recover, with no outside demands. They told me I could stay with them for 6 weeks, 6 months, or forever. I honestly believed I would be fine after just a month of safety. Laughable when I look back at it, but, then again, there are times when I find it hard to be realistic about the immensity of the problem.

The years between 2001 and 2006 were a hard struggle, both for them as they opened their home to me, and for me, as I struggled to find a way to cope with my past. Some in my position have chosen the path of therapy to cope with the traumatic memories of abuse and the adjustment to life in a world of which they have no understanding. I decided not to go into therapy. I chose instead to concentrate on living in the present, trying to come to terms with what most people take for granted.

Up until 2001, I had spent my life cut off from reality, unable to express or accept emotion, with neither experience, nor understanding, of what a healthy relationship was. I trusted no-one. I believed that love was something that hurt, and that it was therefore something to be avoided. On a basic level, I had no self-esteem. I believed that my purpose in life was to be used for other's sexual gratification. I had no concept of body image, no idea of what food tasted like, and no ability to make decisions for myself. The first time Janet asked me what I wanted in a sandwich, I went into a complete panic - firstly because I was being given a choice, and secondly because I did not know what I liked or disliked. I was constantly waiting for someone to hurt me physically, mentally or sexually. I could not understand it when they didn't. I had many moments of complete irrationality, during which I became unreachable. Many times, I felt like a child in an adult's body, as I tried to learn things that even five-year olds knew. Over time, I began to slowly develop emotionally, beginning to feel cared for and safe, though it was only too easy to slip back into old thought patterns.

I felt like I was climbing a mountain but never really progressing beyond the foothills, all the time having flashbacks of memories and fearing that cult members would eventually find a way to persuade me back to that life or carry out the death threats they issued to those who escaped.

My memories of that first year with Janet and Derek are rather fragmented. I remember some things but not all, which, in all honesty, is probably for the best. As survivors of ritual abuse will know all too well, there are certain dates which are extremely difficult to handle. Some of my personalities were badly triggered at these times. My car was with me, but Janet kept the keys as the pull to go back to the cult was so great. During a festival date in particular, our minds would be thrown back into knowing what was going on with the group. We would think we were there, and not in a safe place. Janet would have to stay up all night with us, trying to calm us down and convince us of where we were. One of her favourite solutions was to soak a tissue in lavender and tell us to breathe it in. It did help but must have cost her a fortune in lavender oil!

At other times, I would scream at her to let us go back to the group as I could not cope. This was all part of the programming I had undergone. I was told for years and years that I could never escape, that I would never cope in the world. One day, I was so desperate that I grabbed a kitchen knife and demanded she give me the car keys and let me go. Instead of running a mile she stayed in the kitchen with me (admittedly at the other side of the room). In time, she began to move closer, asking me to talk to her and repeating my name over and over until she managed to get through to me and get me to give her the knife. Not surprisingly, the knives disappeared after that.

After a few horrid festival days, Derek suggested that she and I went away during these times. He believed that if I were physically further away, perhaps I would not feel the pull so much. So, we had several days away in different parts of Scotland, just spending the time quietly going for long walks. We spent one long weekend in a cottage in the middle of nowhere, and only when we left did Janet start laughing. She told me that we could not go back there again, as she had hidden the kitchen knives under the sofa and forgotten to put them back.

It was also during that first year that we got a dog. As I was alone some days when one or other of the other two were at work, we decided a dog would be a good idea. We hunted online for a breed that was friendly but protective, finally deciding on a rough collie. We went to visit the puppies, and there was a tiny male dog that no-one wanted. He was the runt of the litter and seemed to lack in confidence compared to the others. He was the perfect choice. We called him Finn, and he became a really important part of my healing.

Finn loved having cuddles, he followed me around, and boy was he protective! One day, Janet hit me on the arm in fun and Finn was right there. I remember one time when I was alone in the house when a BT engineer arrived out of the blue. He wanted to climb a ladder to check something. At that point in my recovery, I simply could not cope with cold calls from strangers. I was stressed out and afraid. Because Finn was expert in picking up on my moods, he would not let the guy down from the ladder. I felt safe with Finn. He didn't want anything except food, walks, and cuddles, so I found it easy to connect with him. With him what you saw was what you got and I could relate better to him than I could to humans. I have mentioned previously that in human relationships I always felt I had to do what others wanted, as this is how I was trained to behave. With animals it was different. They expected nothing from me. They were not controlling, manipulative or abusive so I felt I could relate to animals in a free way.

I also remember that, during that first year, I felt as though it was safe inside the 5 acres, but that on the other side of the garden walls there were wolves waiting to devour me. I could get quite fixated on this, even though logic told me that there were not really any wolves lying in wait. Probably it was just my fear of cult members.

At some point I developed a lump on my breast and had to see the Doctor. Thankfully it was nothing but an abscess, but during the conversation he asked if I had a social worker. He found one for me who came and visited once a month. The social worker was impressed with what Janet and Derek were doing and tried to support us all. Apart from anything else, he realised that their kindness was saving the NHS a fortune. He suggested, however, that they might want to make it official. That way, they would get paid for having me there. Janet and Derek decided not to go down that road, as they felt that it would put them under the remit of social services, who would not only likely burden them with perpetual paperwork but would also be able to tell them what and what not to do. Nonetheless, the social worker's input was good in the sense that he was trying to support us all. Even though Finn barked at him like mad and one of the cats bit his ankle. He had to run the gauntlet of animals to get to see me!

Out at the back of house was a large piece of land where Derek had tried growing vegetables in a small plot. I remembered that, as a child in England, we had a small garden, so I decided to try my hand at gardening. When I had moved in with them, I had a broken leg. However, as it got better, I wanted to do something physical. I enjoyed it so much that we hired a small digger and went into expansion in a big way. I ended up with about a dozen raised beds, a greenhouse and two 30 ft. polytunnels. I loved growing vegetables, together with wild flowers. It got so big that Finn and I spent all day there, either working or just sitting on a bench drinking coffee. I felt it was a way of connecting with the world. Not only that but watching something grow from seed seemed to go some way towards balancing out all the destruction I had seen in life. Gardening did have its complications, though. Suzie enjoyed it, as she was the one who had enjoyed gardening before we moved to Scotland, and I enjoyed it too. Trish, however, had no patience for it at all. If we weren't careful, something would be pulled up when she grew frustrated with it, which would upset Suzie. The other four personalities were still not engaging with the world.

I started driving again after roughly a year, when things had settled a bit. I remember one day deciding to go into town to do some clothes shopping. For some reason, Derek did not seem too happy about me going. I wanted to go, but it went badly wrong. I met someone from the cult in the street, who triggered one of the other four personalities, who ended up being taken to a house and raped. By the time I had come back to myself, calmed down, and driven home, Derek was seriously worried. He took one look at me and knew what had happened.

To someone who has DID, triggers can be very dangerous. A 'trigger' can be a word, a smell, a sound, or any number of things. The best way I can explain a trigger is as a kind of psychic explosion in the mind. When triggered, we are thrown into a fight/freeze/flight response. We are suddenly thrown back into a memory held by one of us, just as though it is happening in the now, and not in past. During these flashbacks we feel the bodily and emotional reactions of that time. I hate being triggered. I guess that when living with Janet, I went out of my way to avoid anything that would trigger me but, unfortunately, triggers have a habit of jumping out on you. For people with DID, life is like walking through a minefield, always braced for the explosion. The result is that you are in an almost constant state of stress. I have a long list of triggers, I know of, and a longer, unconscious list of triggers I don't (often, I will be triggered but never work out what caused it).

Derek was an architect. As there were several steading buildings, he decided to convert one of them into a small cottage for me to live in. I was interested in the plans, enjoyed watching the project take shape, and helping to decide on colours on the walls. He was not impressed with a fairly dark blue for the bathroom but, when it was on, he had to agree it looked good. For my part, I was less impressed with where a male architect chose to put electric plugs. All went well - until I moved in to it. The place terrified me even though it was just on the other side of the courtyard from their house. It had an atmosphere that I found really negative and, after 2 days of hysteria, I was back in the main house. Janet and Derek's daughter later told me that she had the same feeling about it, which made me feel slightly less paranoid.

As there was a field lying empty, Derek went out and bought two small highland cows. Again, because they were animals, I could relate to that idea. So, when he was away working, I would get up in the morning to feed them.

Life, however, was becoming difficult for Derek, as he was teaching architecture 80 miles away a couple of days a week. All the travelling was becoming a bit much for him. We started to look for a house nearer to his work, but difficulties arose regarding the location. Eventually, a property was found, and Derek spent some time there before Janet and I moved in, sorting out some renovation work.

We finally moved in August 2005. It was in a small village, which was problematic as I did not want to be around people. Nor did I want to lose my huge garden and settle for a small one. Janet was also having her own doubts about whether or not she wanted to move, and if the village was the right choice. I had been living with the couple for four years by then, but the cracks began to show during the move. I didn't want to be in that place, and Janet was confused and unsure. We began to take it out on each other. and Derek had to cope with our decreasing civility towards each other. Trish seemed to be constantly angry, throwing things around the bedroom, slamming doors, yelling at Finn, throwing the laptop around, and basically damaging anything she could get her hands on.

An added factor contributing to our problems was the appearance of a new social worker. Instead of supporting what we were doing, she became a destructive influence. She never once spoke to Janet or Derek. Things with her came to a head when she accompanied me on a visit to the GP, and then took me to a pub for coffee afterwards. In all the years of living with Janet I had not had a drink, and I had never felt the need for one. However, after a stressful visit to the doctor, I ordered some alcohol. When it came to 5pm, I wanted to stay in the pub for a while and take the bus back to Janet's, but the social worker said that if I did not leave with her she would phone the police and have me sectioned. This unfortunately resulted in Trish appearing and telling her in no uncertain terms to get lost, as having a drink was not a sectionable offence. Eventually I rang Derek to come to get us. He was furious, and told the social worker that he thought it was totally unprofessional to take a client to a pub.

The social worker reported the matter to her psychiatrist boss, who, unfortunately, was one I had met back in 1992. In June 2006 I saw him for an interview which lasted 10 minutes before I walked out. Or, rather, Trish walked out, slamming the door behind her. I was accused of slipping under his radar and becoming involved with his social worker. If I slipped under his radar, it was only because his social worker had not told him I had been referred to her by my previous social worker. To cut a long story short, he then felt the need to write a four-page letter to my GP, summarising my psychiatric history and asserting that I had borderline personality disorder. My response was to write back an equally long letter pointing out that he himself had referred me to a psychiatrist who said I had DID, but he had chosen to ignore it. I further pointed out that he had taken quotes from various notes out of context to prove his point. I had lived quite happily without psychiatric input since the 1990's and was more than happy not to get involved with the psychiatric community again. The only thing that this particular psychiatrist and myself agreed on was that psychiatry had done me no favours.

Eventually, I decided that, given the deterioration of my relationship with Janet, I had to try living on my own again. I spoke with my GP, who said it would take probably one or two years to get me ready to move. I ignored her advice. I found a housing association in the next village which had flats and applied. Everyone thought that would take time, but I filled in the application form anyway and very surprisingly I was offered a flat just three weeks later. I don't think Janet thought I would really do it, but I was determined. Both Janet and Derek stepped up to the plate to help me again as I moved. I had nothing except my personal belongings, so they gave me a bed, a sofa etc. My friend Sara (about whom you will hear more in the next chapter) was also very generous and sent me a considerable amount of money to help me buy things like a cooker and a freezer.

So, in October 2007, I moved out - not on the best of terms with Janet and Derek, but at least still speaking. By July of the following year, we were not talking at all. My mother had died, and they did not come to the funeral. Janet said that in view of what my mother had done she would not have come to the funeral even if she had been free. I on the other hand felt that it would have been nice to have had their support. I did not want to be at my mother's funeral either I had no choice, not least because my father had dementia by that point.

Perhaps that is not totally true. I could have chosen not to go but, as usual, I was doing what was expected of me.

Looking back on those years with Janet and Derek I ask myself, did I handle things properly and make the right choices? Hindsight is a wonderful thing. Perhaps I made some mistakes, but I thought my choices were right at the time.

I thought I could draw a line under my past and just move on. I didn't pay any attention to the fact that my history of abuse had left me traumatised. Trauma is such a complex thing, and it affects every part of life.

'Trauma' is such a simple word, but it covers an enormous number of horrible things, all of which survivors have to deal with on a daily basis. The list is long but from it includes: -

- Emotional overwhelm,
- insomnia,
- lack of concentration,
- feelings of numbness,
- loss of interest,
- irritability,
- depression,
- hopelessness,
- loss of a sense of future,
- shame,
- worthlessness,
- little or no memories,
- flashbacks,
- nightmares,
- mistrust,
- hypervigilance,
- anxiety,
- panic attacks,
- pain,
- headaches,
- eating disorders,
- substance abuse,
- feelings of being unreal or not in your body,
- self-destructive behaviour,
- loss of sense of self.

Now I can see that I ignored all of those things, thinking that just being in a safe place would make them all go away. I knew that the past had happened, but I used the same strategy I had used all my life - which was to just keep the memories and emotions locked away in boxes in my head. I don't remember crying about anything that had happened. I did, though, have a general feeling of being worthless, and of not deserving a life, but this was probably because I had been given that message over and over by my abusers. I think that in many ways I was storing up problems for myself which would have to be faced one day.

But in another sense, being in a safe, supported environment seemed important as a way of physically recovering and learning how to be within a 'normal' family. I was not 'cared for' by Janet and Derek but given the space to learn. I watched how they related to each other. I saw how healthy family dynamics worked when their adult children came home. I spent a lot of time watching. I remember, at one family meal in particular, I was watching to see how their son dealt with what was on his plate and tried to copy what he was doing. Derek later pointed out that I should have been watching someone else if I wanted to learn table manners, as his was not a good example!

I tried to learn to trust, but always seemed to be waiting for one of them to hurt me. If they argued, I got afraid, as I was scared of anger. If they had visitors, I went into a panic as I did not know how to relate to them. Having conversations was hard, as there was so much about life I knew nothing about and therefore could not talk about. Did these visitors think I was the 'live in idiot'?

It was Janet who introduced me to reading. I had never read in the past but discovered that it was something I enjoyed. That was a learning experience too. In books, I could read about relationships and emotions from a safe distance. Music, too, became something I got into. I discovered Leonard Cohen in their record collection. Some people say his songs are so depressing, but to this day his amazing words have the ability to cheer me up.

I discovered nature, and not just through gardening. I remember one night being at the beach with Janet when it was dark. For the first time I really saw the stars and heard the sound of the waves. It was almost overpowering. I had walked around all my life in some kind of daze. Yes, I knew that a tree was a tree but I never really truly *saw*. It was like I was in a goldfish bowl looking out and things around me were distorted.

When I lived with them I discovered that I had huge problems with food. My abusers in the past had made me eat things that were not for human consumption, so certain textures or colours of food would set me off into panic and gave me a huge sense of fear. That was something we had to be aware of in order to stop it from happening. But, again, I found ways around it rather than ways to deal with it.

I had always used a shower rather than a bath, but my bathroom in Janet's had a bath as well as a shower. The fact that a bath was there freaked me out. It brought back memories of my grandmother holding my head under water until I felt I was going to drown. Even now, though I can have a very quick bath, it is certainly not enjoyable, and even washing my hair under the shower brings it back and causes me to dissociate.

Perhaps in truth my sense of denial was too great to do therapy, and I did the best I could in those years of living with them. It was an important stage to go through, I think.

Though I have just written about my time with them for over 6 years, there were a few other people in my life during those years, so I was not a total hermit. These two other people became important in my healing process too, but in different ways.

Chapter 4

Meeting Sara

While I was living with Janet we decided to go to a conference on ritual abuse. I was worried about going to something like this, as I thought it may raise memories. I was still in my phase of denial, and I did not want to look at the things that had happened in the past. In the end, I found the conference boring. It was largely just professionals talking about how to raise awareness of ritual abuse, and not about how survivors actually felt. On reflection, I can see there I had a war going on inside me. While I did not want to look at memories, I also wanted to stand up that day and tell them all what it felt like to be a survivor of ritual abuse. Needless to say, my sense of denial came out on top!

Something good did come out of the conference, however. I met someone who was to become an important part of my life. On the journey to the conference, Janet told me that her counselling supervisor would be there. When we were in the car park I noticed a woman in the fairly large crowd outside, and immediately said to Janet – "that's Sara". I have no idea how I knew this - I just had a feeling it was her. I was introduced to her later in the day, and we immediately connected. I felt like I had always known her and, for once, I did not have a problem talking to a stranger. What I had forgotten was that she already had an in-depth knowledge of me due to the fact that, as Janet's supervisor, she obviously knew my story.

All I knew about her was that she had been a psychiatrist and was practicing as a Person-Centred Counsellor in central Scotland. She had her own therapy centre, from which she herself worked, and rented out rooms to other counsellors. I also knew that she had married one of Scotland's best-known prisoners, because I remember the press coverage it got in the early 1980's. I am sure she will not mind me revealing this, as she has recently written a book about her life in which she goes into that time in great detail.

After the conference, we began to exchange e-mails - though I have little memory of what I was saying to her. Unfortunately, my journals and copies of e-mails were destroyed a while ago.

I discovered that she had a Trust Fund which helped people who were in need of counselling and could not afford it. Also, the Fund helped to pay for training courses, and other therapeutic activities. There was a riding stable not far from Janet and Derek's, and I wrote to Sara asking if horse riding – something which

I felt could be good for me - would fall under the category of 'therapeutic activity'. Her response was to invite me to her counselling centre to discuss it. I was thrown into a panic, as it meant a four-hour journey to get there by train. After much persuasion, I was dropped at the train station and picked up at the other end by Sara. We spoke about several things, but not about the horse riding, which rather mystified me. In truth, it probably annoyed me as well. Just before I had to leave to get the train back, I forced myself to ask her about it. Her reply was that she had already begun sorting out the money for me to do it, she just wanted me to realise that I did not have to stay a hermit at Janet and Derek's. I guess, in a sense, that sort of set the tone of our relationship. I always felt like I was one step behind. But in an amusing way!

Sara sent the money to the riding centre, and I went to discuss things with the woman who ran it. She was a firm believer in the therapeutic power of horse riding, and actually reduced her fee so I could have more sessions. Instead of just riding I got to groom the horse, saddle him up, etc. before actually riding. I really enjoyed that, as it felt like I was building a real relationship with the horse. When it came to the riding bit, however, our relationship was not that good. I had not been on a horse for many years. The first time we went out for a trek through the woods, the owner was leading him. I was just sitting in the saddle holding my breath. Eventually I began to relax, and progressed from just walking to trotting, and having what I would call proper, productive lessons. He was one stubborn horse, who seemed to get pleasure doing the opposite of what I wanted him to do. In that sense we were probably too much alike! Unfortunately, I had to give up riding sooner than I would have wanted because of a sore knee which I later needed an operation on. I put my knee problem down to the riding and not to my previous abuse. Yet more denial.

I started to visit Sara on a regular basis. I'd go down on a Wednesday lunchtime and return on a Thursday afternoon. This, however, was not without some difficulty. Janet and Sara had a disagreement over a professional matter and stopped talking to each other. Probably each were as stubborn as the other. It meant, though, that when I went back to Janet and Derek's, the conversation could be difficult, as Janet in particular did not want to even hear Sara's name.

Sara was having her own problems too, as she did not know how to define herself with reference to me. At one point she suggested that she could be my counsellor. She was always of the opinion that I needed counselling. I was of the opinion that I did not. So, for a while, two powerful women clashed on the subject. It felt good to be able to have a difference of opinion with Sara. I felt that our relationship was safe, with no threat of abuse. Therefore, I could say what I thought without fear of being physically or sexually hurt. I explained to her that I liked going to see her to do ordinary things, and, if she was my counsellor, we could no longer do that. I think that in the end we sort of compromised. We would spend some time when I arrived talking about how things were with me, and then the rest of the time we would go for a walk or a meal and just enjoy each other's company. So, although nothing was official, I guess I gave her a little access to the contents of my mind for an hour every now and then. She eventually defined herself as a 'supportive friend', and there is no doubt in my mind that she certainly was. She continues to be supportive to the present day.

At one point she convinced me to see a counsellor not far from Janet and Derek. In a weak moment, I agreed. That lasted for two or three sessions. The counsellor told me that she believed in the physical aspect of counselling. She sat on the floor talking to me and the closer she got physically the more I moved away, until the wall stopped me retreating any further. So that came to a pretty quick end. The whole thing just made me nervous, and I can't to this day understand why she felt the need to be physically close.

When I was visiting Sara, I stayed overnight in her therapy rooms. Once she had gone back to her house, she always told me that it was my space, to do what I wanted to in. The only proviso was that I did not look in her filing cabinets! I spent the time writing, drawing, or just listening to music. I remember one evening we were chatting and she really annoyed me about something. My need for counselling probably! I had a bad reaction and said that if the place was my space while I was there, I would prefer that she was not there. She removed herself and went home. I worried all night that I had gone too far and expected her to return the next morning saying I could not go to see her again. People in general did not stand up to Sara, though I had a habit of it. However, the next morning came and she arrived with an apology for pushing me too far.

My GP at that time said that I had a habit of surrounding myself with powerful women. I would agree that both Janet and Sara were powerful. But I was too, in my own way, because I had survived all the abuse and was still standing.

In other ways, I was not powerful. I could be easily convinced of things that I did not necessarily agree with, and I often got afraid. But with Sara it was fun to give as good as I got, and we had lots of laughs. One day, I was going downstairs to have a smoke, and she shouted something down to me. My response was to shout back that if we were stuck on a desert island together one of us would not live long. She just laughed.

One day, while we were sitting talking, Sara told me that I was very vulnerable. That may be true, but I was not about to admit it. I said that I wasn't. She said that I was vulnerable to sexual approaches because I did not know how to say no. She went on to say that if she made a sexual approach to me I would not be able to say no to her. I have to say, that was a bit of a worrying moment! Did she mean she was about to? Thankfully, she was just making a point in a manner that I could not ignore. She said that it was her responsibility to hold the boundaries so that I felt safe with her and not threatened, as I had been so many times in the past.

I believe she held that boundary really well, as I never felt threatened by her. Eventually, we began to work on my fear of physical touch. She began to move away from just person-centred counselling and did training in physical energy work. I enjoyed trying out things with her.

I think one of the first things we did was with hand cream. Even though I was doing a lot of gardening, I still felt a lot like a head without a body. Because of all the abuse I was cut off from my body. Probably because I didn't want to think about what had happened to it over the years. I had also been told over and over that my body was not mine, but only existed for the pleasure of others, which made it hard for me to connect with my body. So, one evening, Sara brought over some hand cream and got me to put it on my hands, massage it in and see how it felt. It felt strange. In a way in felt alright - but I still was not connecting. So, she put some on her own hands and told me to feel her hands, all the lumps and bumps and wrinkles, and to do it with my eyes shut. The thought of eyes shut was frightening. What would she do when I was not looking? Could I cope with the feeling of vulnerability that arose at the thought of it? I tried it anyway. It felt like an amazing experience. I was truly present in that moment. Not just feeling her hands but feeling my own hands connect both with me and with her.

On another occasion, she took me over to see the new house she had recently bought. On the way there she told me she could sense my anger. I couldn't. However, she would not let it drop, and kept telling me that I was still angry. By the time we got back to her counselling rooms, I was angry at being told I was angry! Was that her plan, or was it accidental? After we had coffee, she said again that I was angry. I was probably bordering on fury by then. She told me to stamp my foot - but I couldn't. Expressing anger was difficult for me. Trish could do it, but I couldn't. Sara stamped her foot and told me to do the same. It was a half stamp so I had to try again. Each time Sara stamped her foot I tried to do it the same way, and with the force she was using. Eventually I got the hang of it. From there, we progressed to cushions. She told me to hit her with a cushion. That was hard too, but, in the end, we were both standing, hitting each other with cushions. Again, it felt good. Like something inside was being expressed but in a safe environment. Every time I had shown any emotion in the past it had been used against me, and I ended up being hurt physically, emotionally, or sexually. But this was in a safe place. Emotion could come out and nothing bad was going to happen.

I went to a workshop Sara was holding about healing. I had never done anything like that before and was quite nervous about what it involved. We started by walking round in a circle with our hands on the shoulders of the person in front. I think I felt I had walked into something 'new-age' and felt like a bit of a twit. The woman in front of me was running the workshop with Sara, and I thought that, if anything, she would pick up on my negative energy. At the end of the exercise she asked - how long I had been a healer? To say I was taken aback was an understatement. She went on to say that I had a very healing touch. Perhaps she said that to everyone, but, to someone coming from my background, it made me feel good to know that my touch felt good to someone else. Somewhere during that exercise, I must have been connecting my mind and my body. At the end of the day we did some dancing to drums, and I found that fun. It was interesting that during the day Sara was always sitting beside me. It helped me to feel safer, because I was being protected from touch by strangers (well, for the most part).

Sara started doing a course of body work which involved working on a person's chakras. I do not profess to understand chakras - other than that we have a certain number of them in different areas of the body, and they can get out of alignment. I agreed to act as a case study for her course. This involved lying on a couch as she held a crystal over each chakra in turn. The crystal is supposed to turn in a circle gently if the chakra is open and aligned. When she held the crystal over mine it was doing seriously strange things, like going around and round in a figure of eight. I assumed from this that my body was basically in a mess. Not hard to believe.

Being a case study for her was another learning experience. After the bit with the crystal, the healing session was very hands on. Starting at my feet, she held her hands over different parts of my body. The first time she touched my feet she said she could feel me pushing her away. Not physically, but with my energy. She was right about that. Closing my eyes and relaxing into it was a near impossibility that first time. I got feelings of panic, my breathing pattern went all over the place, and I kept opening my eyes to see where here hands were going to land next. But somehow the relationship we had developed made it easier the next time. She was probably the first person I trusted to touch me and keep it safe. Sometimes memories would come up during the healing, and Sara could sense it. Actually, sometimes it was pretty easy to sense, as I completely tensed up or stopped breathing. Sometimes she would ask what I was remembering, and sometimes not. Sometimes she would just ask me to look at her as she worked so that I could stay grounded. Even after she finished her training, I would get a session from her when I visited, and I eventually found it really helpful. I was much more relaxed afterwards and felt much more 'in' my body.

After the first couple of years of going to visit her, she suggested that I might like to try going to some kind of Retreat Centre. This, she said, would give me somewhere else to go that was mine, and not involved with Janet and Derek. I had no idea what a retreat centre was. She suggested three different places and wrote down their details for me, asking me to think about it. Her Trust Fund would pay for the first year. I chose the last place on her list based on the fact I thought she had put them in order of her preference. Years later she asked me why I had chosen the last one on her list. I was honest in my reply. She just laughed and said she knew how my mind worked and she had reversed the order when she wrote them down. No much wonder I always felt I was one step behind her! It wasn't a bad feeling though, as every time I took the train home I burst out laughing about something I had said or done but not intended to.

Sara was, and is, a very important person to me. She has been there with her support for the last 15 years. She has not just supported me emotionally, but also financially. Like Janet and Derek, I owe her a lot that I can never repay. She taught me a lot about myself and gave me a safe relationship in which I could explore touch and my feelings.

Unfortunately, because of what happened after I moved away from Janet and Derek (more on this later), my connection with my body was largely lost again. I went back into protection mode to survive those years between 2007 and 2015. But at least my continued visits to Sara gave me the short spaces of sanctuary where at least I could connect again, even if on a temporary basis.

I should say that she had experience of working with people who have DID before she met me, so I was in relationship where I was understood, as were my other personalities.

Sara, and my relationship with her, have not only been incredibly important to me – but have also given me a trove of good memories (much needed in a head full of bad memories!). In writing this, I have smiled several times. We settled on her role as being 'supportive friend' – but in that hour or so of serious conversation we had each visit, I think she actually managed to sneak in a lot of therapeutic content. I think that it is only as I put it in writing that I see that - yet again - I was one step behind!

As Sara remains a part of my life, she will continue to pop up in the next chapters, but I feel it is important to turn now to the part that the retreat centre played in my continuing recovery.

Chapter 5

Joyce

As I mentioned in the previous chapter, Sara offered to pay for the first year of my visits to a Retreat Centre.

In 2004, I made my first trip to the Centre for a few days to see if I liked it. Janet put me on the bus, and Joyce picked me up at the other end. To say I was nervous is an understatement. I tend to form a picture in my head of what someone will look like, and Joyce was nothing like the mental picture I had. She was 20 years older than me, dressed in denim skirt and denim shirt. Her hair looked like she had cut it herself. I later found this to be true, as she only had it cut by a hairdresser about twice a year. The rest of the time she did it herself!

The Centre was about 5 miles from the nearest city, in the most amazing situation. Travelling to it involved driving down through a narrow road surrounded by trees, but suddenly we came out from the trees to be faced by the Centre, which overlooked the water and mountains in the distance. It was a small building in terms of Retreat Centres, with only 5 bedrooms. The first thing I noticed was that it had a feeling of being a home, with no locks on any of the doors and hardly any rules. Except, no shoes to be worn indoors and, no smoking inside. Downstairs had a sitting room with open fire, and a library leading off from it. The kitchen was the domain of the staff, and where visitors gathered for lunch and supper. All the rooms looked out over the amazing views. Above the bedrooms was a sanctuary, where they had meditation for half an hour both morning and evening. Going to this was the choice of the individual. It was an interdenominational centre, which meant that visitors could be of any faith (or of no faith at all). People could go there just to relax, to have a silent retreat, or to attend one of the many workshops they ran. Spiritual direction was offered both by Joyce and by the other person who came to help her run the place. Often, they would have a volunteer there who helped out with the cooking and other domestic duties.

How the place came into being is an interesting story. Joyce herself had been married, with a daughter, and had been a teacher. But after divorcing her husband she felt free to follow a more spiritual path. She met another woman and they began discussing their shared wish to start a Retreat Centre. Many years were spent looking for the right building until, one day, her friend looked out her cottage window and suddenly realised that the steadings building across the road was exactly what they had been looking for. So, the building was renovated, and the Centre opened in 1992. Sadly, the following year, Joyce's friend died, and she was left to carry on with their vision on her own. This vision was to provide a place where everyone would feel welcome and accepted; a safe place for individuals in which to explore profound questions about God, life, and themselves. A place in which, to rest, to be nurtured, and to be restored. She worked there until she retired at the end of 2015, by which time she was over 80. I don't know how she did it really, as she lived in a single bedroom, working 7 days a week. She was truly a jack- of- all- trades, doing everything from spiritual direction, cooking, cleaning, washing, gardening, office work and anything else she could think of. The only long break she had every year was from just before Xmas until the beginning of March, when she went south to her flat there and spent time with her daughter and grandsons. Her life was the Retreat Centre, which must have been hard for her daughter, who was hundreds of miles away.

My first trip there was not too successful. Within an hour of arriving there, I announced that I wanted to go home. As I had never been to a place like that before it basically scared me to death. Plus, there was no television or radio, so I had no idea what to do with myself. I was persuaded to stay the night and see what I felt like the next day. Those first mealtimes were a nightmare. I hated sharing a table with complete strangers, all of whom seemed at ease with themselves and each other. Another complication was that I did not understand most of what they were talking about. My life had been spent either in ritual abuse situations, or effectively cut off from life, so I was not exactly expert in current affairs or different religious traditions! I avoided the meditation in the evening – it seemed a step too far. My idea of meditation was to lean against the shed outside, smoking, while looking at the view and watching the birds on the bird feeder. Often there was a red squirrel feeding on the nuts. To me, that was meditation. Janet phoned Joyce several times to see if I was doing ok. I don't suppose I spoke much to Joyce on that first visit, but I was aware that she had the ability to gradually help me to feel more at ease.

Her approach must have worked, because during that year I went back twice, each time for longer visits. I still found the silence difficult, as well as the fact that I was somewhere 'spiritual'. For the first year, I spent most of my time sitting in the lounge, reading novels, while everyone else seemed to be reading spiritual books. Janet had told me that by reading novels I could learn a lot about life and relationships, which actually turned out to be true. I found spiritual conversations difficult and could not relate at all to talk of God being a God of love. After years of being abused by people who were 'supposed' to love me, I connected love with hurt, and somehow could not get my mind to see it any other way.

At the end of that first year, I explained to Joyce that I could not visit as much because I could not afford it. Amazingly, she said that she would drop the daily charge from almost £40 a day to £15, as she felt it important that I kept visiting.

Gradually, I fell into a pattern of having 5/6 weeks at Janet and Derek's, followed by 4/5 nights at the centre. The more I went, the more our relationship developed, until she came to see me as her Scottish surrogate daughter, and I certainly felt she was like a surrogate mother. Our relationship continued when I was back with Janet and Derek. We exchanged e-mails almost daily. Sometimes just discussing how our days had been, and sometimes talking more in depth. I remember her saying that working at the Centre was strange sometimes. People would come and visit, talking to her in depth about their lives, problems, and struggles, and then return to their ordinary lives. Sometimes she would never see them again, and sometimes she would see them months or years later and not know what had happened to them in that time. I think part of what brought us so close was that our relationship continued during the times I was not there. Also, over the years, she began to talk to me about her life and the problems she had experienced. I felt very privileged that she could do this. Having a two-way relationship felt good.

I spoke more to her about having Dissociative Identity Disorder, and how professionals did not believe in it. I opened up about my different personalities, and I eventually opened up about my background. One thing about Joyce was that she was totally unshakable. This is something that many people have said over the years. Whatever people said to her, she dealt with it in a calm, understanding way. Once, when I was there, a young girl came to stay who had been in a mental hospital. Her mental health worker had visited her one day and found her sitting in the wardrobe. This was deemed by the mental health worker to be irrational behaviour, as a result of which she was sectioned and put into hospital for several months. She explained to Joyce that, in times of extreme anxiety, she would find it calming to sit in the wardrobe. Joyce felt that the mental health services had over reacted and had not discussed things adequately with the girl. She told her that she should feel free to sit in the wardrobe if she wanted, but that it might be an idea to come out for supper. After a few visits to the Centre, the girl told Joyce that those visits had helped her more than mental health services ever had.

What Joyce did was to accept, unconditionally, every person who went there. Not only was she a spiritual director, but she also had qualifications in transpersonal therapy. That, added to her incredible wisdom, made her a really special person. She could judge what people needed or didn't need. On one occasion, I travelled up there by train in a very suicidal mood. I planned to get off the train half way, walk up into the hills, and take an overdose. Janet rang

Joyce to see if I had arrived safely, and when I was not there, Janet phoned me on my mobile - getting angry. Her anger made me worse. Joyce, on the other hand just kept leaving messages. Every message said the same. 'Where are you my love? Phone me and I will come and get you'. Eventually, the calmness got through to me and I rang her. She drove about an hour to get me, gave me supper, and said to go to bed. We would talk about it the next day. Quite often I would arrive upset, and she would just wait for 24 hours until we spoke about it.

She was adamant about only one thing in all the years I knew her. She did not believe I should do therapy. Another person with the same background as mine had been to the centre several times, and one day had brought several painful, horrific memories to the surface. When she returned home, she could not cope, and went to see her psychiatrist. Unfortunately, she lived in the same area as I did and therefore was not believed. Because of this, she was given inappropriate medication, and was more or less told she was lying. The result was that she became very ill and did not get the help she needed. Joyce went with this girl to the Pottergate Centre in Norwich. They specialise in Dissociative Disorders. They confirmed that she had Dissociative Identity Disorder and wrote to the Scottish hospital to this effect. But, as was to be expected, they took no notice of the letter and continued to treat her for an illness that she did not have. Because of that experience, Joyce did not think that therapy was a good idea for me. Nor did she encourage me to talk in detail about what I remembered in case I could not hold things together emotionally. I feel that she was right in this, as my doctors at that time were diagnosing me with Dissociative Identity Disorder one minute and then changing their minds the next. As I just wanted to forget the past anyway, I was more than happy to not talk in depth.

As time passed, my involvement with the Centre increased. Partly because I felt that if I were there on a reduced rate, I should do something to justify my existence. I began by gardening and moved on to being in the kitchen just before mealtimes, washing the dishes. Sometimes I would spend all day in the garden, feeling I had to be doing something. Joyce picked up on this and told me that I did not have to justify my existence, I just had to relax, as no-one expected me to do anything. This did not entirely stop me, though. Occasionally I could even be seen hanging out the washing. Joyce sometimes cleverly made use of my smoking habit by asking to fetch things from the outside freezer the next time I was out for a smoke. Not that she approved of me smoking. We always used to have coffee and share a bar of chocolate in the kitchen before bed, and when she gave me a goodnight hug she used to say it was like hugging an ashtray.

Free from the burdening thought that I had to justify my existence, I started going for walks and taking photographs of the scenery. Often, I would just sit and look at the beauty around me. I developed a love of being in the woods, or of sitting beside the shore, listening to the sea. More and more, I felt like I was 'in' the world instead of feeling like I was in a glass bubble, just looking out but not really being a part of it. Some of the photographs looked quite good, and I came up with the idea of turning them into postcards and notelets, which were sold at the Centre, with the money going into their funds. This was a joint effort between me and Suzie. I did the hard work, and she put stickers on the back of the cards saying they were made by Suzie!

Mealtimes continued to be difficult. I remember one occasion in which the other people at the meal were therapists, counsellors, or healers. I went into total silence and just wanted the meal to end. Later that evening Joyce asked what the problem was. I told her I just felt intimidated by these people who were confident, knew what they were talking about, held themselves with poise, and had impeccable table manners. She pointed out that I had a habit of judging people instantly according to their occupation, looks or conversation. To me it seemed sensible to make my judgements on those criteria. She pointed out that I had to learn to look beneath the surface of people. Everyone had a face that they presented to the world, but that face was not the true person. There was so much more beneath the surface if I looked and listened for it. And, she continued, would I stop being so critical of myself? Because I was as good as anyone was. I think that this was a large part of my problem. Because of my history, I always saw myself as being worthless in comparison with everyone else.

My problem with judging people took years to get over. It raised itself soon after when I decided to join in with a workshop one weekend. It was on the subject of healing, and it occurred quite soon after I had attended the workshop with Sara on healing. The evening before, we had had, a meal during which I took an instant dislike to a female vicar who was there to take part over the weekend. She was confident and eloquent, so I automatically judged her as a threat. The following morning after the introduction, we were asked to go into pairs for an exercise. I sat looking at my feet until Joyce pointed out that someone was looking at me. Just my luck! It seemed that the woman I had judged wanted to pair up with me. We were asked to put our hands on our partner in a place we thought they needed healing. I went into a cold sweat at the thought of touching someone I did not know. And how was I supposed to know what needed healing in another person. She did it first and touched my feet. When sharing with the group after she said it was because she felt I needed 'grounding'. She was right. I never feel grounded. To this day I feel that my head and my body are not really attached to each other. When it was my turn I decided to touch her hands. That seemed the safest option. My hands were hot and sweaty with stress. But when I did it she started to cry. Afterwards she said that my hands had felt really cold and healing. She felt upset because her mother had been a healer and she herself felt she had the gift too. She had denied it because she was a vicar and thought it would be frowned on. Because I touched her hands she felt she should acknowledge her gift and go home and introduce a healing element to her ministry. This involvement with healing workshops was very confusing to me. Firstly, because physical touch had always been painful for me - as the majority of people who had touched me were abusers. Secondly, because I could not understand why people said I had a healing touch. I had avoided touching people for most of my life, as I did not feel comfortable with physical touch.

It was not all serious, though. In September 2005 I met a young woman who was at the Centre for her first visit. Though I was probably old enough to be her mother, we got on really well, and both had a sense of humour. We would be sitting reading quietly in the lounge, and suddenly she would burst into laughter and read me something from a spiritual book that she just found funny. One time, we decided to go to meditation in the evening, but could not look at each for fear it would set us off into laughter. She came to the Centre once a year when I was there, and it was always great to just pick up where we left off. We are still in contact today.

My humour began to play a part. If I could not contribute to serious conversation at mealtimes, I found a way to entertain people with my humour. The only person who could get the better of me in the humour stakes was an Irish nun - who basically had me in fits.

Nor was my relationship with Joyce all serious. We used to escape from the Centre and go out for lunch or have walks. We spent many hours sitting on a rock during lambing season, waiting to see a lamb being born. It never happened. Each morning we went back to discover more lambs, but we never saw one being born in all the years. If she had been really busy during the day, sometimes she would have a glass of wine in the kitchen at 9pm. If someone knocked on the kitchen door in search of milk, the wine glass was suddenly hidden between boxes of cereal which were set out for the next day. If I was there during Wimbledon, we would set up her laptop in the kitchen to watch it in the hopes that no one would come in. If it was a really good match, she would hope that people would not sit around too long chatting over supper so we could get back to it for a while before she led the meditation. Many laughs, and happy memories.

What Joyce provided in particular was the spiritual aspect of my recovery. I knew that the Centre was involved in Ignatian Spirituality, and one day in 2005 I asked her what that was. It is an ancient spiritual tradition that I can't do full justice to here, so I will just explain the very basics briefly. At its root is the deepening of a person's relationship with God, whoever the person perceives God to be. The spiritual director gives the person either a passage from the Old Testament or New Testament. If, for example, the person was looking at some verses from the Old Testament, they would have a period of silence, read the passage several times and see what word or phrase was 'saying something' to them. Then you just explored your thoughts and feelings about it. If you were given a New Testament passage, it would usually be a story. You imagined yourself in the story, and you thought about what feelings and issues were being raised. Afterwards, you spoke to your spiritual director about it, and they helped you to deepen your understanding. The aim is to deepen your relationship to God by recognising where any potential blocks are. Despite the name, spiritual directors do not 'direct' you per se, but they do help you to explore. I am sure that most Spiritual Directors would have a heart attack at my description, but a short paragraph is necessary to explain what I want to go on to talk about. If anyone is more interested in the process, there is plenty about it on the internet.

I started doing these exercises with Joyce in 2005, but I never finished them. They are broken down into four different sections (or weeks), but I only got half way through, as I kept having gaps of about a year when I didn't do any of them. Sometimes I did them face to face with her, and sometimes by e-mail. I actually found them very helpful and, in a way, they acted as a spiritual therapy for me. Recently, I found the e-mails from Joyce in which she responded to my mental wanderings, so at least I have a pretty accurate record of what I spoke about at that time and the issues that were raised for me.

The first scripture passage she gave me to think about was referring to God's love for everyone. Immediately I had problems, as I saw myself as being unworthy of love. Mainly because of what had been done to me physically, emotionally and sexually. I had deep feelings of guilt and shame as a result of these events. My dilemma was that I did not see how anyone (including myself) could love me. Joyce did not have a 'pat' answer to this, but she acknowledged that the reason why some souls come into such a life so fraught with difficulties was beyond her understanding. She pointed out that she knew it gave me a greater depth and empathy with others, but the cost had been too great. After a long discussion about the issues that had been raised, my conclusion was that I felt like I was passing through raging rivers, fire and flames, but I would not be swept away or set ablaze.

Though I had found some inner fighting ability, I was no closer to accepting that I was loved. I had begun a long journey of learning to see myself as a survivor rather than a victim of what had happened.

I made progress in other areas. In taking Finn out for walks, I had begun to notice the world around me. But, at the Centre, I started seeing how things were created in such a wonderful way. The movement of the tides. The birds using the flow of the air. If everything in nature had a place and a purpose, I began to feel that I must have a place a purpose too. I didn't manage to figure out what my purpose was though!

However, I came to see that my problems did not define me. Having mental health problems did not make me a lesser person. I realised that not everyone could accept or understand me. It's not easy for people to understand me when one moment I am acting like an adult, and the next acting and sounding like a seven-year-old or being a 29-year-old who did nothing but get angry. I began, with Joyce's help, to see that even if I did get negative reactions from people, it was due to their lack of understanding and therefore their problem, not mine. I didn't need to wish I was more like Janet, Sara or Joyce. They all had attributes that I didn't have - but I had things that they didn't. Not only did they give me things, but I also had things I could give to them. At times I thought my purpose in life was to improve their levels of patience!

Although I can explain that transition of my thought processes in a paragraph, it took many, many months for it to all sink in. I think that Joyce must have despaired sometimes, as my positive thoughts would slip back into negative ones in the blink of an eye. Plus, having lots of personalities make things difficult. Suzie was more open to the thought of being loved, whereas Trish still has issues with the subject.

I had long conversations with Joyce about the termination I had back in 1986. I still had a lot of guilt and regret surrounding that. Even though my doctor had made the decision and left me with no choice, I still felt that I should have fought harder. At the root of my problem was the fact that I didn't really believe termination to be morally right, and was stuck, unable to move on. Joyce managed to put another slant on it. She said that by having the termination I had saved the unborn baby from being born into a life of ritual abuse. In turn, the unborn baby became the means by which I was eventually able to escape that life. She said that it was incomprehensible at the time, but in hindsight it gained clarity. I could accept the truth in what she said. Had the baby been born, it would have been subject to the abuse I had suffered, the cycle would have continued, and I would never have been free. Difficult to come to terms with, but it did shift my mental position. I would have never have wished what I went through onto my own child, but I know that it would have happened. The cult's hold over me would have been even greater.

I soon came to realise that not only did I have a problem with love, but I also had a problem with power. One of the scripture passage we were looking at referred to a loving and powerful God. This mixture of love and power was not a concept I could understand. My experience was of people having power over me, and love was nowhere in the equation. Ritual cults have everything to do with power, and nothing to do with love. Joyce explained to me that the power of love could be at work. This was totally different from the love of power, which was what cult members had. Gradually, I came to understand the phrase 'power of love' because I saw it in Joyce all the time. Her love was totally unconditional.

I found a paragraph that she wrote to me in an e-mail where she told me to have faith and trust in love and healing. She said that the way forward was to be able to trust love, to experience it within myself so that healing could take place and I would know that I was choosing love in my life rather than hate. She pointed out that I was beginning to feel this happening as I appreciated nature, loved Finn, and was beginning to want the best for the people around me. I think in truth that I learned more about love from watching Joyce than I did from anything else. She was always totally accepting of everyone who came to Centre, treating everyone with the same unconditional love, and doing so no matter how tired she was, or what problems she had of her own.

She had two phrases that she constantly told me. The first was to refer to what she called 'my little wallows'. The first time she used it was when I told her that Janet, Sara and she were pretty unfortunate to be keeping me company during these rough years. Her reply was that 'we are all fortunate to be alongside you so will you please forget that little wallow'. Over the years I had numerous little wallows and many more that were not so little. Her second phrase she used often was to tell me to 'stop putting yourself down'. I still saw other people as being better than me and having more to give. She used those phrases so often she must have been saying them in her sleep sometimes!

In 2006, I became aware that my past was holding me back from my future. The memories I was trying to keep locked inside were not being dealt with. All my energy was going into trying to live with them and keep them under control. It felt like I had them all in locked boxes inside my head and I was using all my strength just trying to keep the lids on the boxes. I was afraid to take them out and look at them in case they shattered my mind, but I was finding it increasingly difficult to ignore them. I looked again at the question of therapy, but still felt that it was not the way forward for me.

Part of the answer, however, presented itself during a trip to the Centre. I saw the memories as a weight which was slowing me down and exhausting me. Over a period of days, I felt I had to somehow find a way to put the weight down. To give it over to the healing power of love. Little by little, I had been allowing love into my life, and felt that perhaps I could consciously place the past into that love. Joyce and I went up to the sanctuary. I lit candles to symbolise truth, faith, compassion and forgiveness. At the centre I placed a candle to symbolise love. I had spent all morning on the shore, looking for the blackest stone I could find, to symbolise the bundle containing the past, and I gave it over by placing it under the candle of love. I sat quietly experiencing what it felt like to have handed over the past, aware that these memories were now sitting under love's healing power. They were no longer things I had to carry on my own. I spent some time allowing the experience to deepen within me and to become a part of who I am. I began to understand how my previous life had been based on negativity, and how negative thoughts about myself were making it difficult to progress. I learned that, rather than getting into the turmoil of negativity, if I could turn towards the love, the negative thought patterns could be broken.

Looking back on the years 2001 – 2007, I had the support of some very special people. Janet and Derek, who provided me with a safe place to live. Sara, who helped me to learn about and accept safe touch. (Not to mention the unofficial therapeutic input that sometimes I didn't even notice!). And, finally, Joyce, who gave so much of herself in her attempt to teach me about love. She was one of the wisest people I am ever likely to meet and was, I think, the first person I truly loved and cared for.

From them all I learned different things in those years, but, reflecting on that time, I can see that my denial and refusal to look at my feelings about the past was very much in evidence. I had fought Sara on the subject of having a therapist and won. Joyce, on the other hand, did not want me to do therapy. Placing the stone as a symbol of my past under the candle of love was helpful and did bring relief. But I was still running from facing the things that had happened. The emotions were still kept in their locked boxes in my mind. My feeling is that during that period I made as much progress as I could. Rome was not built in a day, as they say! Learning about how to live in the world was perhaps all that I could cope with, and what we all accomplished in those years was probably enough of a challenge for me. I am aware that I didn't show emotion when I spoke of things that had hurt, and seldom, if ever, did I shed a tear. That was another throwback from the past. If I ever showed my abusers I was upset and vulnerable, they went out of their way to make the pain worse. I had developed ways of saying something without showing the emotion that went with it, as it felt safer. Though I knew I was loved and cared for by these amazing people, I still did not trust.

Chapter 6

Living on My Own Again

When I moved into my own flat in late 2007, both Joyce and Sara continued to play a part in my life. They were obviously all suckers for punishment. As I write that sentence, I can almost hear Joyce telling me to stop putting myself down!

When I left the safety of living with Janet and Derek, I thought that I would move forward and things would be fine. But I had made a decision without really considering or being aware of the consequences. The years until 2015 became the years that almost totally broke me, and the events which occurred not only stressed Sara, but almost broke Joyce's heart too.

I soon ran into problems with coping on my own. I either forgot to eat, or I would dissociate because of the stress of deciding. Kitchens have always been difficult, as Trish really does not have an interest in food, and Suzie (being only 7) was not to be trusted. Often, I would turn on a ring on the cooker, only to dissociate. Whoever took over would wander off and do something else, unaware that the cooker ring was on. Plus, food was, and still is, a huge trigger for me. My GP was considering meals on wheels as a solution, but the local coffee shop came to my rescue. I had been there a few times even though I had been warned about them by the local minister. It was run by evangelical Christians, and the minister said that they caused harm to several people. She said that she had picked up the pieces of people who ended up in a worse state after the ministrations of these evangelicals. Their belief system held that, if you were mentally ill, all you had to do was to repent, and give your life to Jesus, and all would be fine. Unfortunately, the flipside of this was that if people were not fine then they obviously had not repented enough! Personally, because of my visits to the retreat centre, I had a much wider view of spirituality. However, I argued that I could look after myself, so the minister agreed that I would probably be ok going there for coffee.

I spoke to Victoria, who ran the coffee shop with her husband (who was the pastor of their group), and she gave me a voucher for £10 each day so I could go there for breakfast and lunch and take something home for later. I appreciated that, as it gave me more freedom than meals on wheels.

But that freedom ended up being a bad experience for two reasons. Firstly, evangelical Christians have got a habit of seeing the devil at work in everything.

Victoria herself had suffered from depression until someone told her that an old family clock had evil spirit in it! They burned the clock, and she was fine after that. From a personal viewpoint, I would beg to differ. Victoria and her husband decided that I did not, in fact, have DID - but was demon possessed. I was persuaded to go to a meeting to be exorcised. Where on earth was my brain? Needless to say, they got a very verbal Trish, who point blank refused to repent of anything and certainly was not in the mood for giving her life to Jesus. They took the refusal to say the name of Jesus as proof of possession. I was rescued by Suzie, who said it, and we all beat a hasty retreat home.

Secondly, despite the aforementioned 'exorcism', I ended up spending most days there - and Victoria was getting overly friendly. She would sit with me many times when she was not busy, and she started rubbing her leg against mine under the table. Again, I found myself in the position of being uncomfortable, but unable to say no. She was texting me in the evening. Sometimes up to 20 texts a day, all of which were phrased in a way that needed a reply. Again, I was thrown back into my previous programming, so was unable either to not reply, or just switch the phone off.

Part of my tenancy agreement with the housing association meant that I had to have a key holder in case of emergency, and Victoria offered to hold my spare key. The result of this was that she could (and would) arrive at any time of day, even letting herself in after I had gone to bed. Several times, I awoke from sleep to find her lying on the bed beside me. I think the most worrying part was that she seemed to be preying on Suzie.

I had made another friend, Mary, whom I met in the pub one evening. She became very wary of what was going on with me and the people at the coffee shop. Mary was down to earth, sensible, and we both had the same weird sense of humour. She introduced me to her family and became one of my best friends. One of the down sides of having DID is that I am unaware of what happens when I am Suzie, Trish or one of the others. Mary, however, had relationships with Suzie and Trish, so often could tell me things that I was not aware of. Suzie would tell Mary of the presents that Victoria had given her and how Victoria liked to give her cuddles. Mary tried to tell me that what was happening with Victoria was not good, and that the situation was becoming dangerous for me, but I couldn't do anything about it. The old programming was still there. I couldn't say no to things, and I felt I always had to please everyone.

During the late part of 2007 and early 2008, I was going into the city once a week to see my father. We had lunch together, and then visited my mother who had been in a nursing home with dementia for several years by this point. She could do nothing for herself, and she needed total care. During one visit she took my hand and called me darling. As it was the first sign of a loving gesture from her it totally freaked me out. I couldn't get my hand back quick enough.

As I always went to visit on the same day, it was not hard for members of the cult to know my movements. Several times I was on the end of verbal threats. These ranged from telling me that I would never survive without them, to actual death threats. They were obviously worried that I may be a threat to them. I suppose I could have stopped going to the city but, though I felt nothing for my mother, I did have feelings for my Dad. I felt that I could not leave him on his own - and besides, what were verbal threats anyway?

In early July of 2008, I was in the coffee shop when I got a phone call from my mother's doctor, saying that she had a chest infection and did I want her taken into hospital. As I held the Power of Welfare for her, I made the decision for nature to take its course. Dad and I sat with her for 2 days until he decided that he had enough and went home. It took a further 2 two days for her to pass away, and afterwards he refused to go and say goodbye to her. I rang Mary, and she came to help me to organise the funeral arrangements. The nursing home staff took me to see my mother and told me to take my time. I stood against her door, totally confused as to what I was supposed to feel. I actually felt nothing. No grief, no pain, no relief. Just nothing. The minister where I lived did the funeral and, for some unknown reason, I decided to read from the Bible. A passage about love of all things! By this time, Dad had the early stages of dementia, so did not really understand what was going on. When the people were leaving the crematorium, two men I did not know came up to me. They said that they had worked with Dad, and that they wanted to be there for him. I thought there was something strange about that, as Dad had retired 25 years before. It bothered both Mary and I, but I thought nothing more about it.

Not long after that, however, things took a very distressing turn. Mary and I would go out for a drink once a week and, as we lived at opposite ends of the village, we made our way home separately. One evening I was walking though the square where there is a car park. Suddenly, a car door opened and I was pulled in. The shock brought on a switch of personality. When I got home, it was obvious I had been raped. While I was living in that flat, there were two rapes, numerous threats, and times during which, according to Mary, I disappeared for several hours. I would return unable to say where I had been or what had happened. Each time I was raped, I sent a text to Mary and to Victoria to see if one of them was free. Victoria always wanted Mary to go home, saying she would take care of me. One time she showered me, and another time she took me back to her house. Her husband was there, but she got Suzie and put her in the bath, washing her and telling her she loved her. This seemed to become a pattern. Bathing Suzie, wrapping her in a towel, and then lying in the bed with her.

We went away for two weekends. Once, Victoria was going to a Christian conference and invited us. She did not, in fact, attend the conference, phoning her husband to say it was not what she expected. So instead we spent the weekend going shopping, having meals out and, at night, she shared a bed with Suzie. The second time, a group from the coffee shop went to a Christian convention and we were invited. Again, she managed to organise the hotel rooms so that Suzie and she shared a room.

Suzie continued to tell Mary what was happing. Victoria would come around, and Suzie would lie with her head on her lap. Victoria bought a baby bottle and filled it with milk, feeding her like a baby. All the time telling her over and over, I love you. The inevitable happened when the bottle was given up for the genuine nipple. Mary told me that Victoria was using Suzie for sexual gratification. As for me, I wasn't even there while all of this was occurring, though I can believe that sexual feelings had something to do with it. If Victoria had been away on holiday, she would almost come to mine straight away, and the fact she was trembling and breathing strangely told me that sexual feelings were increasingly coming into our relationship.

It was during that time that Mary and I went to the retreat centre for a couple of days. Joyce invited us out for lunch. Before Mary had a chance to take a mouthful, Joyce asked her what she thought of Victoria. I think Mary almost choked! She told Joyce her true opinion of the matter, and Joyce's reaction seemed to confirm that Joyce was uneasy about it too. Mary felt that Victoria was using brainwashing tactics on Suzie by the constant repetition of 'I love you'. Perhaps Suzie had said something to Joyce which had raised her suspicions.

During my time of going to the coffee shop, I started having coffee with another woman who went there. She was married, and also had mental health problems. One day, I got fed up with drinking coffee and said I was going to the pub. She came with me. Not long into the conversation she said she was bisexual, and that she fancied me. When I left to go home, she asked if she could come too. It was obvious what she wanted. Because I was taught to give people what they wanted, I did it. Afterwards I was in a terrible state, and I told Mary what had happened. Mary spoke to the woman, saying that I was vulnerable and could not say no so would she please back off. She did.

Not long after this, things came to a head. Victoria's husband got suspicious because she was not where she was supposed to be, but rather with me. Victoria booked into a hotel for a few days and came back to tell her husband what she had been doing. She had to go in front of the trustees of the coffee shop and confess her sins and repent. Her husband wanted to ban me from the coffee shop, but the trustees said that if he did this then they would close the place. From that point on, I did not go there as much, and she backed off from the physical touch except the occasional hug. What really bothered me was that she had to confess to the trustees that what she did was wrong, but never did she or anyone else apologise to me.

Again, I found myself incapable of ending the relationship with Victoria, and just went along with going there for coffee and talking to her. She always wanted to know what was happening in my life, and I always ended up answering. Even when I moved to the other end of the country, she still kept in touch, and I went to see her when I went back up to visit. This continued until my most recent visit, during which I finally saw the 'light' and knew that I would never see her again.

A few years before I moved south (about which more later), I finally saw that what she did was abusive. To take advantage of a seven-year-old personality who didn't understand what was going on cannot be considered anything other than abuse. I got in touch with the police and spoke to them. They were really nice, but at the end of the day decided that they could not bring charges. In the eyes of the law, Suzie did not exist as a physical being, but as a part of me. It took a lot of courage for me to go to the police, but the result of my efforts was a renewed feeling that people could do what they wanted to me, and nobody but myself would be held responsible.

Apart from the incidents of abuse and threats from cult members, I was also having personal problems. The year after my mother died, I was diagnosed with cancer, and the following year my Dad died. It felt like there was just stress piling up upon stress. Let me explain:

Let's start with my cancer. Initially I told my GP that I was not going into hospital for a hysterectomy, but I reconsidered when she told me that without the operation I would be dead within 2 years. Nothing like a reality check to make me change my mind. I have a huge fear of hospitals, because they involve having things done to me, physically. Mary came in with me the night before, and my GP requested I have my operation first thing in the morning, as she thought I would either be too stressed waiting, or that I would walk out in panic. I was so stressed that I could not even remember my last name, and, after the operation, I was put into a single room. Mary later told me that I had been so stressed that they thought I could not cope with a ward. My only interest was in getting out as soon as possible. I had the operation on Tuesday, and I was home on the Friday. I think I dissociated my way through it, as my memories of my recovery are not too clear. I do remember the frustration of not being able to go out other than for short walks, and of having both Victoria and Mary doing my shopping, cleaning etc. At least if I was at home I was not being abused. I felt really sorry for Mary, as she was trying to help me get through the operation and her sister had just died of cancer a matter of weeks before I was diagnosed. My Dad by this time was in a care home with dementia, and I felt I could not tell him. I didn't know if he would understand, or if he would get upset if he did understand. I did not see him for about three weeks, and then Mary drove me to visit him.

During my recovery, I went to the retreat centre. One evening, as Joyce and I were having coffee, she said she had something to tell me. I remember her words. She said she could not let her surrogate daughter go through something without her going through it too. She told me that she had breast cancer, and that she had to go into hospital. She had not told me until she knew that I was ok. As usual, she was putting other people before herself. I think that I coped ok and was supportive. However, on the train home I rang Mary and asked her to meet me at the train station. I sat in the pub with her in tears. The fact that Joyce was ill had a much deeper effect on me than my own illness. Thankfully, she was ok, and got the all clear five years later. I got the all clear in three years. We had both been lucky.

Six months after my operation, my Dad fell in the middle of the night and broke his hip. It caused an immediate deterioration in his dementia, and when I visited him in hospital I did not recognise him. He did not know me, and he was in distress.

For four days they gave him nothing to eat, because he was supposed to be getting his hip sorted but they kept cancelling the operation. Eventually, I was told that they had found that he had bone cancer as well as prostate cancer, and they wanted to treat his cancer before the hip. Finally, I got a doctor to talk to me who said that, given the circumstances, just sorting the hip was the wise solution. By this time, he was 90, and I agreed that getting him back on his feet was more important than cancer treatment. But his health had deteriorated so much that when he was transferred to the cottage hospital for rehabilitation it was thought he needed a nursing home rather than a care home.

To this day, I am sure that he heard and understood this conversation, because he stopped taking his pills and stopped eating after that. I spoke to Joyce, who agreed that he was making his own decision and that I should tell him it was ok to do what he thought was right. Again, having his power of welfare, I took the decision to let nature take its course.

That decision was so very hard, but I believed that he did not want to carry on the way he was. I sat with him every day. So much so that the nursing staff kept telling me to go home, as he did not know I was there. His level of distress was really difficult to see. I had a trip to the retreat centre booked, and the staff told me to go, as it would be several weeks until he passed away and they were trying to keep him comfortable. I told him that I would see him in three days, and the nurses said that they would ring me early the morning if there was any change.

One morning, when everyone except Sue (a volunteer) was at meditation, my mobile rang and I knew that it was bad news. He had passed away. For once, I cried. Cried for him and cried because I was not there. Joyce came down from meditation and just hugged me, saying she had felt half way through meditation that he had gone. I wanted to get on the first train home, but she convinced me to take a couple of hours to let it sink in before I left.

I rang his brother in England, who was so upset that he could not even talk. Again, Mary helped me with the funeral arrangements, and it was her minister who took the service.

I decided that I wanted to do the eulogy. I practiced it at home, but I could not get through it. Joyce asked me to send the order of service to her and told me that they would go to the sanctuary at the time of the funeral, so they could be with me in thought. Sara also knew the time and told me that she would be sending love. Mary and her husband came with me and sat with me, as they were the closest people I had to family there. All the way through the service I kept thinking 'I can't stand up and talk'. The funeral director had told me that if I was in trouble, just look at her and she would save me. Mary sat holding my hand, giving me a bottle of water to drink.

When the minister asked me go up and do the eulogy, calmness came. I suddenly felt the love of Joyce and of Sara coming my way. Mary told me that I was brilliant, and that my voice was steady, calm and heartfelt. That Dad would have been proud of me, as would Joyce. We headed off back home, went to the pub and I drank the quickest pint ever.

During the time that my Dad was dying, I was at Mary's one Saturday and her husband was playing music. One song was called 'Going Home' by Runrig and, listening to the words, I decided that Dad should go home to England and have his ashes scattered in the churchyard where several of his brothers and his parents were buried. His ashes were actually put into his parent's grave, which was really emotional, but I will come back to that as it was a real part of my healing.

Chapter 7

The Police and Mental Health Professionals

If I remember correctly, it was around 2009 that the police first got involved. Sara had been very concerned about what was happening in my life. She had a way of getting me to talk so that when I saw her I would tell her what was going on. She had experience of this kind of thing, and she knew people who came from a ritual abuse background, including people from my area. She wanted these people stopped from doing what they were doing to me, but I was not willing to give names. I was heavily into self-preservation and did not think that going to the police would help. I thought that it would actually make things worse. After several conversations in which I refused police involvement, I was persuaded that the abuse had to stop, and agreed to talk to them. She came up to my flat so that she was there while I spoke to them. Mary was in the kitchen so that she could pick up the pieces when Sara left. I don't remember much of what I told the police, except for the fact that I kept it pretty general. I spoke in general terms of the hierarchy of these groups, in general terms of what they did, and in very general terms of where they met. I found out that they had been investigating reports from other people of a similar background, and they promised that whatever I said would be kept in strict confidence within their investigating team. That turned out to be untrue.

I think that what happened between 2010 and 2015 with the police and mental health services deserves a chapter to itself.

By early 2010, everyone was getting more concerned about the assaults, and Sara in particular wanted me to get back in touch with the police. I was not happy with this idea as I felt that the people who were watching me would only make matters worse if they found that there was police involvement. Sara, however, was convinced that I had to talk to them for my own safety. I gave her permission to get back in touch with the original police who had come to see me, and she sent me a copy of what she had said to them. In her e-mail, she had mentioned several assaults, and said that I had only finally agreed for contact to be made to re-assure others. I still felt that police involvement was dangerous. Perhaps some of my reluctance had been because I had been brainwashed into never telling. But most of my reluctance was because I felt it would only make matters worse. I also knew that most of the people involved in ritual groups come from perfectly respectable backgrounds and are often in positions of authority. They are extremely good at appearing to be upstanding citizens in public, despite being sexual perverts in their hidden lives. They are also very good at covering their tracks.

At this time, I was waiting for a move into sheltered housing as there was a manager on duty there, and it was therefore felt that it would be a safer environment for me.

At the end of April 2010, I was at home waiting for visit from the Minister and his wife to finalise arrangements for my Dad's funeral. When my doorbell rang, I assumed that it was them arriving early. However, it was two detectives who asked if they could come in and talk about 'trouble'. As my neighbour had been having problems with the police, I assumed that this was what they wanted to discuss. This was an obvious conclusion because downstairs had a security entry system, so I assumed that they had been to my neighbour first as they did not ring up to my flat. I later found out from the manager that they had somehow managed to by-pass the usual security arrangements and gained access.

Once inside by flat they started asking questions about the assaults and the cult. Even when I explained that I was waiting to arrange Dad's funeral, they continued with their questioning, and only left when they were asked to do so by the Minister's wife. I felt their whole approach was aggressive and their questions inappropriate especially when they continued to question me at the front door, showing me copies of e-mails that Sara had sent to the original police. Not only was I upset with their timing, and their unannounced arrival, I discovered that they were from a different police area. This meant that the original police had not kept their word about confidentiality. Their total lack of sensitivity and 'bully boy' tactics meant I refused to see them again. Trust is a huge issue for survivors of abuse, and I certainly did not trust these two.

In March 2011 Sara contacted the original police. The abuse had been getting worse. By this time, I had been moved into sheltered housing, but I had my own front door. The doorbell rang one evening and when I answered, two men were there. They pushed me inside and raped me in the hallway, threatening me about how things could get worse. The only way to survive a lifetime of abuse is to switch off. People may think that all these things would have had me crying, in hysterics, or completely crazy. But when a person has been subject to so many traumas, they react in ways that other people would probably not see as normal. I could be assaulted or abused and my mind would switch off. The emotions I should have felt were quickly put into a box inside my head with a padlock. The facts and the emotions were separated. After each incident I would go to bed and, my mind would automatically switch off. I would get up the next day determined not to be beaten by what was happening. The downside was that I could tell someone that I had been raped without showing any emotion at all. It was almost like I was talking about the weather.

Several days after this, Sara asked me to e-mail her the dates of recent assaults. At that point I had not told her of the rape, but I put it in my e-mail. What I didn't realise at the time was that she was sitting in her house talking to the two police who had arrived, unannounced, on my doorstep ages before. She rang me later to tell me they were on their way to see me, and when I threatened to disappear she advised me to stay where I was as they would find me anyway. I was far from happy with this turn of events. I went to Mary's, to raid her fridge of lagers. I have never kept drink in my house and I was in desperate need of something to calm me down.

I thought that I had plenty of time, as they had a four-hour drive to get to me from Sara's - but they sent two other CID to find me. Both Mary and I were taken to the city. They wanted me to have a physical examination. They let me have a smoke before going in and it was during that time that my two 'favourite CID' arrived. As one particular DS needs a name, I think Dick would be appropriate! They often claimed that they had never seen me switch personality, but Mary said it was obvious that Trish took over at that point, asking them what the F… they were doing there. They would not let Mary stay with me. but took her off to police headquarters to interview her. As a 'vulnerable adult' they should never have done the physical examination without me having someone with me. If the way I was treated during the examination is normal procedure then it is no wonder that people do not report rapes. I felt like a piece of meat, having samples taken from just about everywhere with no explanation or conversation. I was then interviewed for at least an hour, where I doubtless said little, and what I did say was without emotion. Mary, on the other hand was interviewed for two and a half hours, being asked if she believed me and if she had ever seen me switch personality. She answered yes, continually, to both, and was shattered by the time we were eventually allowed to go home.

They came to take a statement the following day. Again, I was with Mary, so this time I felt I had someone with me until Dick took her away to talk to her and left me with his woman colleague. Case of good cop, bad cop.

They put a CCTV camera outside my door, took Mary's fingerprints and mine. They said they sent a forensic team into my house while I was at the hospital being examined. Whether they actually did or not remains to be seen. Months down the line, they said there were no fingerprints in the house except mine. Very strange as Mary had been there, as had other friends and, a new kitchen had been put in only a few weeks before. Either all these people wore gloves, or I was a seriously good cleaner!

They went around the town where I lived, asking questions of my neighbours, and visited the pub where I used to drink. They went to Victoria, asking if she had seen me switch personalities. They rang Janet and said they had to talk to her urgently. As Janet did not know what was happening, she was rather taken aback, and did not feel happy answering questions over the phone. Lots of what she knew about me had been said in the confidential situation of counselling anyway. She later told me that she felt bullied and pressurised, but she was firm that she would only talk to them in person. They did not show up for the appointment anyway, so she was relieved at not getting involved. At least she understood my unwillingness to talk to police.

Initially, the police were helpful and polite. But their continued presence was annoying me They visited me several times and I was not comfortable with that. As CID they arrive in smart black cars, wearing dark suits. They just look like CID, and I felt that I was abused and assaulted more because of their presence. The men who were assaulting me did not know if I was talking to the police or not. I felt the situation was being made more dangerous for me. I gave them descriptions of the men involved, but I held out on a name. The people who were assaulting me were just basically thugs paid by the cult in money or drugs to do their dirty work. Even if the police had found them, they could not have led them to the people at the top. I think police, certainly at that time, were ignorant of how things worked. Or were they? In fact, I don't think that they were ignorant at all.

In October 2011, Dick came to see me and explained that they were worried about the stress I was under. Would I be willing to see a psychiatrist who could help me to deal with some of it? Since the late 1990's, I had only seen one psychiatrist for 10 minutes, and I was not keen on seeing another one. However, I agreed because I thought it may help, and Dick was pretty persuasive. Turns out that it did not help at all. Quite the opposite. I had been told by my GP who made the referral that I would be seen by the consultant psychiatrist for my area, but I was actually seen by a junior doctor, who was on placement with the consultant and did not have good English. So, we started with a communication problem. The report he wrote after seeing me twice set the scene for the police attitude that followed.

Basically, he told me that he did not believe in DID or ritual abuse. No surprise there then! He concluded that I had Emotionally Unstable Personality Disorder (borderline). The assaults were part of my elaborate paranoid belief system, which fluctuated with reference to my stress. He suggested I was put on antipsychotics. After seeing him twice, he left for another placement, and I saw the consultant psychiatrist. If I thought she would be more open, I was mistaken. I should point out that this hospital had a real problem with diagnosing DID. I heard of others who faced the same disbelief as me. The consultant psychiatrist told me that there was no such thing as DID, and that she did not believe in ritual abuse. Her explanation was that I had been dissociating and because my mind had experienced a 'gap', I filled in the gap and thought that I had been assaulted. She said I was actually self-harming. Considering that she did not believe in dissociation, I found it strange she was using the word dissociating to describe what she thought was happening. When I dissociate, I have no memory of what has happened. I know that another personality has taken over and I have never felt the need to fill in the gaps. As far as the incidents of assault were concerned, I could recall the detail, and describe the perpetrator. There were occasions of assault of which I had no memory, but I saw the injuries. I did not fill in the gaps then, but accepted something had happened to another personality, of which I knew nothing.

Among all this disbelief, one GP slightly cheered me up. I had a knife wound to my right hand. The GP who was on duty that day asked me if I was left or right handed. When I said I was right handed she asked why, if it was self-harm, had I used my left hand to cut my right hand and not the other way around. It felt good to know that there was at least one professional who was thinking about it. Sara, meanwhile, was really upset and angry at the turn of events. She sent a long letter to the consultant psychiatrist. I think I mentioned that Sara had been a Doctor, a psychiatrist and a therapist who had experience of DID and ritual abuse. She said that the police had been investigating these activities over the past couple of years, including cases which have involved other individuals with similar background, who live, or have lived, in the same area. She therefore found it frustrating and upsetting to see the psychiatric report which appeared to discount this possibility, as well as imposing a diagnosis which could well cast doubt on my ability to recount truthfully the nature of what was happening to me. As far as I know, she never received a reply.

Things came to a head in February 2012. Dick and his female colleague arrived at my house in the late morning. He said he was not there to engage with me, but he told me to go to the police station with them. No-one spoke on the way. I was taken into an interview. No recording was made of what was said and no statement taken. I wrote what had happened immediately after and still have a copy of it.

He said I was to listen, and to talk only to answer his questions. He asked what benefits I was on and how much I received each week. He said that I had manipulated my GP into getting these benefits for me. I had in fact had the benefits for many years before that particular GP.

He said that I had never been diagnosed as having DID, or anything else, and as a result was not entitled to benefit or to be living in sheltered housing. (My medical records say otherwise)

He said that things had to stop. He said that he had had doubts from day one that I was telling the truth, but now it had to stop. He said that he could handcuff me, take me through to the court, and I would be charged. Then he would let me out on bail until it came to court. This would ruin my reputation, as people would know about it. He further said that I was terrifying people in the town I lived in as they believed that an attacker was on the loose. However, now people did not believe this to be true.

He did not think that taking me to court was the best thing for me. He said that there had been a meeting with police, ambulance service etc, and they all stated that there were no injuries. (Very strange, as the injuries are documented). They said that forensics had found nothing in my flat, and there was no sign of violent rape having taken place. I did not actually describe a violent rape but had described how I knew from past experience not to fight.

He told me that I was not a vulnerable adult. He said that the alternative to court was for him and me to go and see my GP. He said that he would not talk during this appointment but would listen while I told my GP that I had been lying. That if the GP put me on stronger medications, I was to take them.

Furthermore, if I phoned the police again, he would arrest me. If I did not answer my front door to him, he would gain access through the housing manager.

He said that if I agreed to see my GP, he would not arrest me, but he said that he could change his mind, and that he had an arsenal of weapons he could use. Asbo, court, social exclusion order etc.

This interview lasted the best part of three hours. Most of the threats came when he took me outside for a smoke and there was no witness to what he said.

At the time, I was not aware that I could have walked out of there at any point. I spoke to a retired policeman I knew, and he said that, as procedure had not been followed, I had actually been free to leave whenever I wanted. The truth is that the guy was terrifying me with his talk of arresting me, and I was in pure panic. I agreed to see my GP with him because I honestly believed he could arrest me. Though he never did say what he could charge me with.

He phoned me on the Saturday of that week to 'see how I was' and asked if I had rung anyone on the Friday evening. I said that I had phoned Joyce and told her. Frankly, she was horrified. He told me to stay at home, relax and keep safe, and that there was no need to phone anyone else. I did later phone Sara who was also horrified.

I told him during the interview that he obviously believed what he was saying. However, I did not believe that I was lying. I maintained that the injuries were real, documented and not self-inflicted.

He rang my GP, made an appointment for us to go, and told me in no uncertain terms that unless I told her I was making it up and doing it all to myself, he would have me arrested. Thankfully, he was held up in traffic, and rang me telling me not to see the GP without him. But the time of the appointment came and he was still not there, so I went in by myself to see her. My GP had the practice manager with her, and she was not happy about the appointment. She asked if I was there under duress from the police and I said yes. When he eventually arrived, he knocked on her door. She went out and said that he could not come in. We waited and the receptionist checked his car had gone. My GP advised that I go to the pub for a drink in case he was waiting for me at my door. So, they let me out the back door of the surgery and I went for a drink till I felt he had given up.

I later put in a complaint about how he had behaved through my local MP, helped by Sara, but when I asked what was happening with the complaint, they said they had lost it. Dick's boss had spoken to him, and he apparently believed that Dick had been acting in my best interests and trying to support me. So, while I was falling apart, he was in the process of getting a promotion.

The CID disappeared from my life, which was no great loss to me, but after being admitted to A&E on several more occasions, the local police took to showing up wanting a statement. When I ended up in hospital I would say that I had been assaulted because I was not about to lie and say it was self-inflicted. But it was making life difficult. After a nasty cut to my head, the police showed up in the middle of the night at my house. I shut the door in their faces. They continued to come back daily, saying they would keep coming until I gave a statement. I failed to see the point in giving statements if they held the view that it was all in in my imagination. After several visits from them in the late evening my GP said to tell them that they should not be talking to me without a 'responsible' adult' with them. But they ignored that and just kept coming.

Another time, I was being kept in hospital overnight due to having banged my head as a result of being pushed down an embankment. The police showed up at the hospital in the middle of the night to apparently 'be nice' and give me a lift home.

My GP of 10 years said during this time if she thought all my injuries were self-harm, she would personally lock me up and throw away the key! It is well documented in my records that I do self-harm, but never anywhere other than my left wrist. In a sense, my GP's comment made me feel a bit better, because at least I felt she believed that the injuries were not self-harm.

I was living a life of fear and was constantly looking over my shoulder to survive. Not only was I afraid of being assaulted, but I was afraid of the police and what they could do. This situation continued until my return to England in 2015.

I thought long and hard about writing the last two chapters, because they are not about the process of recovery, and are pretty negative. But I decided that they were important to include. Recovery is not all positive. It has a lot of negative aspects, and I think it is important to acknowledge this. I don't think I would have survived through these difficult years had it not be for the continued support of Joyce, Sara and Mary who were integral in helping and supporting me.

People who have been abused for a long time develop certain patterns of behaviour. They have no self-esteem, and they feel worthless. They feel that they cannot say no. Basically, they are traumatised, and go in into fight/fear/freeze mode when they feel threatened. They do not have a sense of self, and they find it hard to make decisions for themselves. Pleasing other people is more important than standing up for themselves. In fact, they don't know how to stand up for themselves. Instead of living, they survive, in any way they can. They turn the hatred that should be directed towards other people inwards. Self-care is extremely difficult, if not impossible.

Matters become more complicated when extreme trauma leads to Dissociative Identity Disorder as a result of ritual abuse. There are many people out there like me who have come from that background. To manage to get away from it all is a victory, but the price is huge. Many like me have had the same problems with health professionals. From what I have heard and read, many do not get the right diagnosis and, even if they do, are not offered the help they need. It gets even more complicated if ritual abuse is mentioned. It is still not accepted by health professionals or by the police. Often, the police themselves have members who are involved, and survivors are threatened into silence. When we are denied the help we need, we begin to question our own sanity. We believe the cult members who said that we would never survive or be believed in the outside world. It can drive us to the edge sometimes and we feel like giving up.

But if we have the strength to escape the abusers' grip, we have the strength to survive.

I know that people reading this who are the same as me will understand. Perhaps these two chapters may go a small way towards helping others to understand the problems we face.

These years of the last two chapters were not all negative. If they had been, I would not be sitting here writing this. I was fortunate. I had the love of Joyce, Sara, Mary, Janet and Derek. They never once doubted, and they were there to pick up the pieces during times that I could not take any more. Their belief and love were what kept me going when I felt that I couldn't keep going. So, in the next chapter I will return to how their love helped me in the process of recovery.

Chapter 8

Healing Continues

Had it not been for the continued support and friendship of Mary, Joyce and Sara, I do not think I would have made it through those years. Because of them, my healing was continuing.

Another factor which helped was that gardening came back into my life. After Dad's death, my GP got in touch with a social worker who got me a placement where I went and gardened one day a week. It was a small community where several people with learnings disabilities lived. They also ran a day workshop for people. Activities included renovating old tools, woodwork, craft activities and gardening. They had several co-ordinators who led the teams, and I became involved with the gardening team. The gardens were large and beautiful and I got on really well with the gardener. It was the kind of place where you were asked what you wanted to do rather than being told what to do, which was really helpful for me. I felt that I had a choice, rather than feeling controlled. This was important. Being back in nature helped to keep me 'grounded', and the physical exercise was good, too. The advantage with working in the garden was that I could work on my own and not be surrounded by people with whom I would have had to make conversation. We all met up in the large kitchen for a shared lunch, which was more difficult, as being with more than a few people was quite stressful. However, I found it easier to trust those with learning disabilities. They tended to be more open, and therefore I knew where I stood with them.

The social worker eventually managed to secure funding for me to go twice a week. I should say that my GP had referred me to an ordinary social worker rather than a mental health one. I only saw her twice a year, when she came to do a review with myself and the gardener to see how I was getting on.

In the winter, we went into the craft room, and I started off by doing knitting. The gardener was multi-talented, and she knew lots of crafts. Mind you, her attempts at getting me into the kitchen to try baking were not too successful. Because my stress levels kept rising, she eventually put an onion in front of me and asked me to draw it. We then went on to try and see if I could draw flowers and attempt to paint them too. I was looking through a book of paintings one day and passed the comment that Van Gogh's painting of the Sunflowers was worth millions but looked simple. She put a canvas I front of me and said to paint it. It was actually great fun - though I did discover that it was not that simple at all! I enjoyed being creative, and so did Suzie. Though, again, Trish did not have the patience. Those 2 days a week spent in a safe, relaxing environment helped me to cope with the other things that were going on. Just being there felt healing.

Also, I was getting to know Mary's family at a deeper level. None of them had a problem with me having DID, and Suzie loved playing with the grandchildren and with Mary's dog. Mind you, when Trish got angry, the dog disappeared. Finn, my own dog, used to do the same. Being connected with a family again was good, and I learned more about healthy family dynamics. Mary and I went away for the weekend several times, taking the dog with us. Sometimes, we stayed in a caravan and went for walks beside the river, or among the mountains. Just being in nature was relaxing and healing. The relationship I had with Mary was a two-way relationship. We both helped each other through problems. Though we could talk seriously if need be, we developed the habit of laughing our way through problems. This gave us both a bit of relief from things we were coping with in life. Her husband was a lovely guy, who accepted that I had DID but asked no questions. He said he saw me as the elder sister he never had, and he was a man that I felt comfortable with and not threatened by.

My visits to the retreat centre continued every 5/6 weeks, and my relationship with Joyce deepened. I felt more at ease talking to her, and I think I can say she was the only person I completely trusted. I continued to do the Ignatian Spiritual Exercises, but, because of what was happening at home, I often felt unable to do them for long periods of time. It was hard, sometimes, to transition from my emotional shut down state at home to trying to be open and trusting when I went to see her. I think I managed most times.

We spoke lots about love. I came to realise that it was only through love that healing could take place. She taught me that if I only accepted love at a 'head' level then it would not go deep enough. Trusting and loving someone else is a first step, but the next step was for me to trust and love myself. I am not sure even today that I have reached this point. Because I do not know what all of my personalities are doing, it is very difficult to trust myself. And loving myself is something I struggle with daily. Joyce said that I was beginning to come alive and inhabit my body (and the world) in ways that had been shut down before. But it was just a beginning. When we spoke, she often asked me how something made me feel. She encouraged me to go inside my body and see what feelings were there, rather than just thinking about feelings in my head. If I said that I was afraid, for example, she would ask where in my body I felt the fear, and she would get me to try and to describe the feeling. I still struggle with this. I can say that I feel suicidal like I am describing the weather. The fact is there, but the emotion is not.

Because I had been told all my life that I was unworthy, I still felt the same way most of the time. She explained to me that so often it is easy to play the old tapes of my unworthiness rather than listening to my inner voice that was actually telling me something else. She encouraged me to watch for when this was happening. If I heard the old voices inside, she said to try and make a note, and see if I could turn on a new tape. The more I could become aware of the old patterning, the easier it would be for them to no longer have any power. I learned that, unlike the people from the past, unconditional love does not coerce, force or threaten.

She spoke a lot about being 'centred' and 'grounded. I think that when I started going to meditation, I began to feel what this was like. Initially, 30 minutes of meditation felt like an eternity, and my mind would not be still. I would be mentally making lists of things I had to do. I would get frustrated and could not relax. It was hard to stay physically still. Eventually, after numerous attempts, I reached a point where I could still my mind and just become aware of breathing. Instead of breathing in a shallow way because I was stressed, I learned that by managing to breathe deeply, my body would relax as well as my mind. I discovered that if I did not feel 'grounded', I was much more open to negative thoughts. As a result, the doubts would begin to infiltrate, and I would return to old negative patterning. It became important for me to be aware enough to spot the change happening before I got drawn back into the old thought forms. I could manage to do that at the retreat Centre, but back at home, with all the assaults going on, it did not take long to get swamped by negative thoughts. But at least I was learning that it was possible to change my thinking.

I remember talking to her about other people's eyes. How someone looked at me was something I have been aware of for most of my life. An abuser looks with coldness. They look with an expression of pleasure when inflicting pain. They look with hatred. All negative expressions. I also had problems with the way most professionals look at me. They are saying words which sound understanding but the expression in their eyes is not the same. I used to say that their words and their eyes did not match. Therefore, I could not trust them. I remember reading what one psychiatrist had written about me. He said I made no eye contact during the session. The reality was that he had been looking at his notepad and writing all the time, so it was him who was not making eye contact. Joyce said that there was much to learn from how people allow you to look into their eyes, or not, as the case may be. Some people are afraid of being seen – afraid that they will be exposed by another's gaze, and that they might be found wanting. She said that when people live a life of love then what they offer is that care and love that does not seek gratification for itself. They can listen whole heartedly, and truly do care, and are interested in what you say.

We spoke about relationship. Until 2001, I had not really allowed myself to be open to relationships. I would talk to people but did not have the caring feelings to go with it. I don't want to think that if a friend had been knocked down by a bus and killed in front of me, I would not have felt anything. No friend ever was in that position, so I don't know for sure what I would have felt. But I was so cut off from feelings and emotions that I am pretty sure my reaction would have been one of nothing. Joyce and I would talk about our relationship, and how it was deepening. She said that true relationship was equally good for each other. It was not just one sided. Each person, through the relationship, then had the potential to grow more fully into who they actually were. It was only in 2009, when she was diagnosed with cancer, that I realised the depth of love that I felt for her. I felt a concern for her that I don't think I had ever felt for another person. Yes, I had deep feelings for my Dad, but they were mixed up with the feelings I had for my mother and what was happening in my family.

I still had a huge fear of rejection. I thought that if I trusted someone and loved them, I would become vulnerable. Being vulnerable in the past had always led to being hurt, emotionally, physically or sexually. Because of this fear, I was afraid to speak 'my truth' for fear of being rejected. I would agree with things I did not necessarily agree with, so that I would not be rejected. But in order to break away from old patterns, I had to be able to say what I felt. We had many a conversation on this subject. Joyce asked me to look at why I felt I did not deserve love or have the freedom to make my own choices. She said that doubting my own worthiness was such a big block to being able to accept myself. She said that now I had freedom of choice to make my own decisions. It was, therefore, important that I began to look at the reasons behind my inability to say no to people. Everyone has problems with saying no in certain situations, so it is not a problem unique to me. But it did seem that I could not say no to anyone. I guess I had been brought up to obey people, to do what they wanted. I had not been in a position to say no back then, as the consequences would have been dire. I still felt the need to please people and give them what they wanted. I was especially afraid of saying no to people I saw as being powerful. Power still terrifies me. If someone powerful told me to jump, I would ask 'how high'.

Blame, guilt and shame were all feelings that I still had. I felt guilty because I had been abused. I felt ashamed because I had been abused. I felt that I was to blame for it all. Though Joyce tried to convince me otherwise, those feelings still kept popping up. I blamed myself for what the police did. I blamed myself for being convinced by Sara to talk to the police. I blamed myself because health professionals were not listening to me. I think I practically blamed myself for existing. Joyce pointed out that, by blaming myself, I was in fact saying that everyone had more power than me. In terms of the abuse, they did have more power. But in my 'new' life, no-one had power over me. It was important for me to learn that I did not have to do what other people wanted. Important that I learned how to decide and state my decisions without fear of repercussions.

Again, I could work on this at the retreat centre, but when I was at home, facing being assaulted and threatened, it was difficult to stand up for myself. Especially when I was fighting threats from the cult, the police and the mental health services. Even someone without mental health problems would be struggling with all that!

In early 2009, I discovered that the retreat centre was to be running a Spiritual Directors course, and I discussed with Joyce if I could do this. She said yes, and, fortunately for me, Sara offered to pay the course fees (which were quite expensive). The course ran between July 2009 and May 2010. I think that going to the retreat centre for several weekends during this period for the training really helped to maintain my sanity. It was during these months that I had cancer, Joyce had cancer, and my Dad died. In fact, I missed the first weekend of the course due to being in hospital having my operation.

The course itself was really interesting. We learned about Ignatian Spirituality, and about what was involved in being a Spiritual Director. The reading list was pretty extensive and, in between attending the course, there was much to read and essays to write. The role plays were pretty terrifying. We had to practice being a Director with several people watching. They then gave their thoughts on how we had handled different situations. I learned a lot about myself during that time. I found that I was actually capable of listening to someone with real empathy rather than just coming out with the correct words. I had to look at my reactions towards others. After each role play, we had supervision to discuss what feelings had arisen for us. As Joyce was my supervisor, it was pretty hard to pretend that I had not been judgemental, when in fact I had been. I think that the most useful part of the course for me was having to look at myself. To look at why I was afraid of certain subjects that came up, why I was judgemental, why I wanted to give advice rather than just listen and be where the other person was. I also had to face what I thought about myself. Often, I would be playing the role of Spiritual Director, and found myself losing my concentration. I would start wondering what the other person would think if they knew my background. Also, I would feel that I had no right to be doing the course as the old "being worthless" problem would keep coming back. On the positive side, I saw that I had at least one thing in common with Joyce. Pretty much nothing I heard shocked me.

At the end of the course, I got really good feedback about how I had done, which helped me a lot in terms of self-esteem. I had been thinking for several months about how I would like to be a part of the retreat house team. I started to look for sheltered housing that was closer to the retreat centre. Some I went to have a look at with Joyce, and some with Sara. However, none of them were really suitable, either financially or geographically.

Doing the course did give me more confidence. Often, at lunchtimes, Joyce would have her lunch on her own and leave me to serve out the meal to other guests. Up until that point, I was always happier if Joyce were there, as I did not have to make any effort. Now, I had to make the effort, and found it was alright. At supper times, when Joyce was there, I found that people would often discuss personal issues - especially if there were only the three of us round the table. When I asked Joyce why this was, she said that it was because I was allowing the other person the space to open up by just being present. That too was different. I used to be so nervous that others probably picked up on it. Now that I was more comfortable in my own skin, it made it easier for others to open up.

I began to put into practice what Joyce had said in the early years. To look beneath the surface of other people. I began to be able to pick up on how a person was feeling. I could see tension in body language etc. Instead of being judgemental, I could just accept people for how they were. I would often sit at the supper table just listening to how Joyce responded to other people. She was totally present in that moment. She could draw out people who were quiet, but also know and respect it when that person just wanted to be quiet. If someone was talking to her about a problem, I would inwardly guess how she would respond. Sometimes I got it right, and sometimes I was seriously wrong. When we had coffee in the evening, I would often discuss her responses. Just watching her was a serious learning curve for me.

The person I was at home was not the person I was becoming at the retreat centre. I felt more whole and complete there. I felt I had a purpose. I felt I could give love and understanding to others. My dream to actually work there began to deepen. So much so that I was discussing it with Joyce, who thought that my dream was a valid one, and a dream that could come true.

But, in 2013 we both sat down and had the difficult conversation. Although I was functioning at the retreat centre, I was not functioning at home. The daily difficulties I was facing meant that my problems were not going away. I was not going to be healed so long as the assaults were going on. If I did move nearer to the retreat centre and try to work there, my own unresolved issues would get in the way. It was a really painful conversation to have, and seeing a dream go up in smoke is heart-breaking. Joyce was upset, because she saw the potential in me that could not be fulfilled. I was upset, because she had put so many years of effort into helping me, and I felt that I had let her down.

I was still continuing with my visits to Sara, and sometimes she would come to the retreat centre when I was there. As I had a totally different relationship with both of them, I found it quite stressful the first time Sara came to visit. But seeing them both together actually made me realise how much they were both doing for me. Joyce was my spiritual teacher, and Sara my body teacher. They both helped me to work on my mind and emotions. I continued to have the body healing sessions with Sara. I found that, the more I relaxed into them, the more they helped. It was important with the assaults that were going on that my body was given a chance to be touched in a healing way. I began during those sessions to be able to speak about things that were raised for me, but, again, the emotions were still cut off. She never pushed me to open up, but I knew she would listen if I did. For me, it was just good to be touched in safe ways, knowing that she would never overstep my boundaries.

Chapter 9

Decision to move to England

After my Dad died in 2010, I spoke my Uncle in England. My Dad and my Uncle had been very close, even though they had not seen each other for several years. My Uncle asked what I was doing with his ashes, and when I said that I was coming down to scatter them in the churchyard he told me that he was pleased He felt that my Dad should be with the rest of his family, who had passed away before him. He suggested opening Dad's parents' grave and putting his ashes there – but he was also firmly of the opinion that Dad's final resting place should be my decision. I felt that the idea was good. I said that I wanted to read a poem at the graveside, and my Uncle told me that this would be lovely – so long as the poem was shorter than the Eulogy had been! (I had sent him a copy of the funeral service in Scotland, as he was unable to come due to his failing health.)

Mary came with me, and we took the train to England. We joked our way down, saying that Dad was cramping our legs as the urn was in a bag on the floor between us. I was happy to joke my way down, as I had not seen my family for about 10 years, and the whole trip felt stressful. Part of my reason for not visiting my family for so many years had been the fact that both my parents had had dementia, which tied me to their nursing homes in Scotland, somewhat. But I have to admit that my absence from family gatherings in England was also partly because I did not want to explain to the family why I had been living with friends and was not working.

I thought that when we put the ashes into the grave there would just be the Vicar, my Aunt, my Uncle, myself, and two cousins at the graveside. When we got there, I couldn't believe what I was seeing. All my cousins and their husbands were there, even one I had not seen for 50 years. I found it very difficult to hold myself together. If I had thought that the funeral was emotional for me, it was nothing compared to what I felt that day. Even though Dad had not been back to England for over 25 years, they had all come. Also, it felt like I was surrounded by the family who had accepted and loved me as a child. I managed to read the poem, but with a struggle. Mary had to poke me in the ribs as I forgot to lower the ashes into the grave. Afterwards, we went back to my Aunt and Uncles', for a feast that my 2 cousins had prepared. Took me a couple of years to realise that I had not offered to even pay for it. Later, Mary and I went to the churchyard, and she sang the Runrig song. I ended up in tears. It was one of the few times tears had managed to come. Though we only stayed for a couple of days, it felt as though I had reconnected with relatives. I remember during that visit my Uncle asking me why I was not working, and Mary telling him that I was rich and didn't need to work. Though he did not believe it, he did not pursue the subject, for which I was grateful.

I began to visit my family again, and I spoke with my Aunt and Uncle on the phone. However, the following year, my Uncle died - which again had a huge effect on me. I went to the funeral. Sara gave me the money for the fare, which I really appreciated.

As a child, I had been close to my Uncle's daughters, Sharon and Lynn. I saw them when I went to visit with my parents and they came to Scotland on holiday several times. Now, when I started to visit England again, I found myself torn. I did not want to talk about what had happened in Scotland, and that meant I was not being 'real' with them. I was not ready to say anything just yet, though.

Just after my Uncle's funeral, Lynn, who was the same age as me, asked me what I was doing for Christmas. I usually spent Christmas with Mary and her family. Lynn invited me down. I accepted, and that started a pattern. That first Christmas in England I spent with Lynn and her family. She had 3 daughters and numerous grandchildren. My Aunt had been living with them for several weeks as she had been in hospital. On the Boxing Day, they took my Aunt and me back to her house, and she settled in well.

I went to England twice a year after that, staying with my Aunt, and spending time with my two cousins. It was lovely listening to old family stories that my Aunt remembered. It also represented valuable time away from Scotland and what was happening there. It felt like I was back with my roots. But some conversations were difficult. I spoke with my Aunt about my mother and my grandmother. But only going so far as to say that they did not like me, and my grandmother did not like adopted children. I remember one day Sharon came to take me out for coffee, and her self-locking car doors sent me into a panic. Without thinking, I said that the sound reminded me of a police car. When she asked what I knew about police cars, I think I said a quick sentence about being assaulted and got off the subject pretty quickly.

In a lot of ways, going to visit them was difficult, as I couldn't be truthful with them. They knew that something was not right, but I couldn't go into it.

For as long as I can remember, I had always wanted to return to England. When my Dad retired, I asked how he would feel about us all returning to England. My mother said no, and Dad said that it was too late. Another time, I told Dad that I was going back to England, but he asked me to promise to stay in Scotland. He said that if anything happened to him, there would only be me left to look after my Mother. I made the promise he wanted me to. Why? I have no idea, really. If something had happened to Dad I certainly would not have looked after my mother. I didn't feel that it was fair to ask me to make the promise. But, as usual, I did what others wanted me to do. Also, I did not want to leave my Dad there on his own. Throughout everything, he had been as much under the control of my mother and grandmother as I had. Though not with the same results.

After Dad's death, I was looking on the computer at flats for sale or rent in England. Just looking, but not doing anything about it. I was still living in fear in Scotland, but the mind-control that ritual abuse groups use is a powerful thing to break away from. I still believed what they had told me - that I would never get away, never make a life, and would be drawn back in one day.

As the assaults increased and my experience with the police and mental health services went wrong, I still looked for flats in England, but was afraid. What was I afraid of? I think I was more afraid of me than anything else. Could I make the move? Would I manage to make a life? Could I break free from the thoughts the cult had put into my mind? In one way, I thought that if I moved I would be letting them win. I thought that if I stayed in the area I was giving them the message that they could not break me down. Also, I was giving out the message that one day I might talk and name people, bringing them to justice. But what happened with the police and mental health services made it perfectly clear that they would tear me apart on a witness stand.

By this time, both Joyce and Sara were of the opinion that to move away was my only option. I started to look more seriously for somewhere in England, somewhere close to my cousins and my Aunt. I felt it was important that I chose an area I was familiar with. Because of my dissociation, I can get lost easily in unfamiliar places and end up miles away from where I should be. Unfortunately, getting a council property would be impossible because of long waiting lists. My only option was to buy somewhere. I did not think that privately renting would be an option, as there was no security. Private landlords can give you a months' notice should they decide they want to sell the property. I did not have much money, so found I was restricted in my choice.

I spent hours searching on the internet, and Lynn went to view one property for me but said it would be no good. Eventually, I saw a retirement flat on the market which was not far from my Aunt and decided to take the train down to view it. However, the night before I was due to go I went into a complete panic. I am still not sure what caused it. I rang Mary in an emotional state and she came to pick me up and took me to hers. By then I was hardly able to string a sentence together and she had to ring Sharon to say I could not come. I remember feeling totally trapped. If I could not go and view the flat, did that mean I would be stuck in Scotland forever, always experiencing more of the same? I came pretty close to suicide, and I think it was only Mary and Joyce that pulled me away from it.

It was then that fate took a hand in things. My Aunt's health was failing, and I got a phone call to say she was in hospital and not expected to last the night. I knew that she had been ill, but this was a complete shock. She died two days later. As I was close to her, I felt that I had to go to the funeral. My cousins almost reduced me to tears when I ended up with them following her coffin into the church. That they wanted me with them was pretty emotional. Sharon said that her Mum would have wanted it that way.

The following day, Sharon asked if I wanted to at least have a look at the village where the flat was for sale. When I said yes, she replied that we may as well view the flat to get it 'put to bed' once and for all. I saw it, and I liked it. A few hours later I put in an offer and, after a bit of negotiating, the following day the offer was accepted. If I had gone back to Scotland I would have probably got myself into a state and done nothing about it.

Joyce and Sara were really happy. Mary, on the other hand, was upset, as she would be losing her best friend to the other end of the country. However, she put a brave face on it, and admitted that it would be for the best. I think I put in the offer in March of 2015, and then it was just a case of waiting for things to be finalised. Joyce came down to stay for a weekend. She had never seen where I lived before and it was good to have her there. We went to Mary's for a meal, and she met Janet and Derek. She also wanted to go to the coffee shop to see the people there. The timing of her visit was great, as she was there on the day that I heard the contracts had been exchanged. We went out for lunch to celebrate, and for the first time she told me to have a pint to celebrate.

I remember Lynn telling me that her Mum had died to get me down there. That was taking it a bit too far, but I knew what she meant. It was only because of her funeral that I was able to go and view the flat.

The next couple of months went in a blur really. Because I was so busy trying to organise the move, I had to cancel my next visit to the retreat centre. That was incredibly sad, as I never really got the chance to say goodbye to the place. I knew that I would never be back there, because by that time I knew Joyce was retiring. I would not travel from one end of the country to the other if she was not there. She was, however, moving closer to her daughter, and we spent some time poring over train timetables. We discussed her coming to visit me, and the possibility of me going to visit her.

I went and said goodbye to Janet and Derek. We talked about the past, and about how far I had come. I spent time with Sara, knowing that I would not see her often in the future (though we would keep in touch). Her generosity, again, was amazing. When I had moved into my own flat in 2007, she had sent me a considerable amount of money to buy things with. This time, she offered to pay my removal costs, which I gratefully accepted. Her financial generosity was incredible, but it was always her generosity of spirit which meant most to me. Sometimes I did not see her for months. She travelled a lot, to far-flung countries like India, Nepal, and too many other places to mention. She was also busy professionally and personally. But I always knew that she was there for me, and that, when it was possible we would meet up. We kept in touch by e-mail and phone calls.

I saw my GP for the last time. She gave me a hug and said 'get out of here before we both cry'. Probably they would have been tears of relief on her part. I saw the psychiatrist and told her I was moving. She pointed out that I would take my problems with me, and that mental health services were not as good in England as they were in Scotland. I decided to be polite and thanked her for all her help. Her reply was that she had not really helped at all. I admit that this was about the only time we were in total agreement about anything!

Eventually, everything was ready for the move. I put my car on a transporter and got it taken down a week before. No way was I driving a really small car all that way! I think that the whole thing became a reality when Sharon's husband sent me a photo on my phone of my car sitting in their driveway. My reaction was 'oh my God, this is really happening!'.

My furniture was loaded up, due to arrive in England the next day. Sharon would be there to let them in. I spent the last night with Mary and her husband. The following morning, Mary and I got on the train. She was coming down with me for the first week to help me unpack and get settled in.

I think I was working on auto pilot, and not sure that the move was actually happening. I had given no real thought as to how it would be. I did my usual in terms of thinking. I thought I was drawing a line under the whole experience of Scotland and that, when I arrived in England, everything would be fine. Turns out that - although I would be physically safe away from Scotland - emotionally, things were only just beginning.

Chapter 10

Physical Safety in England

Mary and I arrived at my flat to find all the boxes and furniture already there. Sharon had also given me some things which had belonged to my Aunt, and her husband gave me a sofa a chair which had belonged to his mother. Because I really can't stand being surrounded by chaos, I immediately starting emptying boxes and basically putting stuff anywhere, so long as it was out of my sight.

The first week passed in a reasonable way. Having Mary with me made things easier. We went and explored the village and ate in the pub most evenings. We looked in the village magazine for things with which I could get involved. She took me shopping for food and basically tried to help me get organised. I went to see my new GP to get medication organised and had my first surprise. He had received a letter from my previous GP giving a brief outline of my problems. We read the letter together after which he explained to me that he did not care what labels I had been lumbered with during my chequered history with psychiatry. He would not, he said, read my records when they arrived. Rather than be blinkered by the previous, contradictory opinions of his medical predecessors in my case, he would learn about me as a person, and help me with any immediate difficulties as they arose – for now, he would help me to settle into my new community. Personally, I found that rather refreshing. To be treated as a person and not a label made an empowering change.

After a busy week, Mary returned to Scotland. I dropped her at the train station, had coffee with Sharon, and came home.

Being alone in the flat felt strange. Part of me could not believe that I was actually there. Another part of me questioned the wisdom of what I had done. I realised that every other time I had been in England I had been on holiday, and I had stayed with relatives. Now, I felt as though I had landed on an alien planet.

It was also the first time in 15 years that I had owned a property. My old difficulties surfaced. Owning somewhere meant that I was responsible for any repairs that needed addressing. I soon remembered that this caused me huge stress. I was constantly waiting for something to go wrong. A dripping tap would bring on panic. The flat became an emotional danger zone and remains so even to this day. This means that it does not feel like a safe space and therefore I am hardly ever relaxed.

Just over a month after moving here, my GP referred me to the anxiety and depression team, who in turn referred me to someone else. As a result, I was referred to Rethink (a mental health charity). I saw one of their support workers once a week to go shopping. Shopping for food has always been a problem for me. I can't deal with choices. For example, if I want cereal, and am presented with a variety of choices, my mind just goes blank. I can't read what it says on the boxes, and I panic. If I have someone with me, they can narrow down the choices to two or three, and eventually I can choose something. But making that choice alone – something that most people can do easily - would be impossible for me. Unfortunately, even if I buy food, most of it ends up being thrown away. Kitchens and I just do not work in harmony. Trish is not interested in food. Suzie can't cook and needs to have things she can just grab and eat easily. My four other personalities who were always involved in the abuse setting do not know how to cope with everyday things. As for me, I walk into the kitchen and promptly dissociate. Also, food and kitchen knives trigger me.

During the last four months of 2015, I employed my usual coping strategy: ignore feelings and get on with it. I honestly believed that, now I was physically safe, all of the problems would go away. You would think that by now I would have learned that this approach does not work. However, it was the only approach I knew, so I fell back into the old, well-worn pattern. I joined an exercise class and a walking group, brushing away any issues which arose. But I realised that I was dissociating a lot. More than a lot, really. I could not remember who people were, or what we had spoken about. I knew that I was pushing myself too hard, and that my stress levels were rising.

My cousin Sharon got a puppy and, as she and her husband worked on a Thursday, I went to dog sit. Going into theirs on a Wednesday and staying overnight gave me a break from my flat once a week, and also meant that I had two home cooked meals a week. The rest of the time I seemed to be surviving on cheese sandwiches and tins of beans. Plus, the pints of lager that Trish saw as her equivalent of food.

I spent time with my other cousin, Lynn. She had organised a BBQ shortly after I arrived. I thought that it would be just her family, but she had invited all my cousins as well. That meant that there were lots of people. Too many people mean that I dissociate more, so, though it was a lovely idea and enjoyable in many ways, my memories of it are rather fragmented.

That first Christmas, I spent the holidays with Lynn. Again, it was enjoyable in terms of getting to know her family, but it was also stressful. Most of the stress was caused by my fear that I would switch into my child personality. It was ok if Trish was around, as she sounded pretty much like me, so I felt that people would not necessarily notice much of a difference. Keeping up with conversations was difficult, but, because I have dissociated most of my life, I have ways and means of covering up the fact that I have sometimes not heard what is said to me. If I "come back" half way through a conversation, I tend to just listen to what the other person is saying until I get the general idea of what the conversation is about. That can cause a few problems though. It often gets pointed out to me that I have just contradicted an opinion I gave earlier. As I get older, of course, I can use the "senior moment" excuse!

Both Sharon and Lynn knew that I had mental health issues, but I was not prepared to go into any detail. The main reason was basically that I did not want to talk about it - but I was also afraid that they would not understand. Besides, I also had the idea that if I did not talk about it then, somehow, it would all just go away.

I was physically recovering from the assaults in Scotland. I was also putting on weight. Both Sharon and Lynn were really good cooks, and Trish was coping with stress by drinking. Not copious amounts but enough to keep her stress levels down. Suzie has never liked it when Trish has had a drink. If Suzie pops up after one of Trish's sessions, she feels drunk, and she hates feeling drunk. We all have different levels of tolerance for alcohol, and Suzie can feel drunk after just one drink.

So, in a nutshell, the last 4 months of 2015 were spent in denial. Denial that my experiences in Scotland had happened. Denial that anything was emotionally wrong with me. I was in England, I thought, and therefore everything would be fine.

In January of 2016, I went back to Scotland for 3 weeks to visit Mary and her husband. While I was there, I also visited Janet and Derek, and went to see Victoria at the coffee shop. Although it was really good to see friends, I made a few mistakes. I should not have gone to see Victoria as it raised some issues for me. Also, going to my old local pub brought back serious memories.

A few weeks after my return, I ended up being taken by ambulance to the A&E, where I saw the community psychiatric liaison team. I actually have no memory of this, but I do have the letter they sent afterwards, detailing what we had spoken about. I assume that Trish had been the one doing the talking. In the letter, they identified goals, and supported a referral to the community mental health team. These goals included developing a trusting therapeutic relationship. They also identified a need for support with the activities of daily living. They wanted risk management and a social care package put in place. I note from the letter that I made good eye contact, engaged well, and had a sense of humour. These words were to become a pattern in future dealings with the psychiatric liaison team. I always make good eye contact because I find it easier to read a person by their eyes than by their words. When I was being abused, my abusers would often say words that sounded alright but their eyes would be full of hate. Eyes can also mock a person. Eyes can show that an abuser is enjoying the pain they are inflicting.

In March, I had an appointment with Maike (pronounced My-Ka), a recovery care co-ordinator. I was really nervous about meeting her for the first time. So nervous that I don't remember what we spoke about it. I just had an impression of someone who seemed human and who listened. I do remember that her words and her eyes said the same thing. It was decided that she would come and visit me at home every two weeks. Because she treated me like a person and not as a label, I began to open up with her. She met Suzie and Trish and didn't bat an eyelid. She believed in DID, which I guess put me at ease. She was not denying my reality. After years of bad experiences with the NHS, her reaction to me was quite a relief. But I still had doubts. Speaking to her about the abuse I had suffered made me feel vulnerable. I had learned from an early age that shows of vulnerability were a precursor to getting hurt. If I showed fear when I was being abused, my abusers would find that a 'turn on', and they would hurt me more as a consequence. Actually, if I showed any kind of emotion they would hurt me more. I very soon learned not to show emotion, but this had its downside too. When I spoke to Maike, I could say the words, but I could not show the emotion behind them. Everything came out in a matter-of-fact way, even though, under the surface, things were beginning to feel anything but matter of fact.

In Scotland, I had kept lots of memories locked in boxes in my mind, as it was the only way to survive. Now, these memories were beginning to surface - whether I wanted them to or not. One day, when Maike came to visit me, I decided that I wanted to open up with her and tell her that the abuse had been ritual abuse. I told her that I wanted to say something, but that I would not look at her until I had finished. I was afraid that if I saw the slightest doubt in her eyes, I would stop talking. So, I sat and explained some things to her, and then looked to see what her expression said. She asked me if she looked any different. I remember telling her that either she was a good actress or she believed me. It turned out that she had already come to the conclusion that I had been involved in ritual abuse. She believed that such things happened, and she believed me. After the years of disbelief in Scotland I could have burst into tears. Needless to say, I didn't!

In May, I had another trip to A&E. I was really upset one day, so I drank three quarters of a bottle of wine and intended to overdose with pills. I rang Maike in an attempt to stop myself. So, another conversation was had with the psychiatric liaison team. Needless to say, I made good eye contact and had a sense of humour. While I was able to talk with Maike without using my defensive smile and sense of humour I found (and still find) it hard to drop defences with professionals I do not know. Actually, I find it hard to drop the defences with most people.

In early June, I met a psychiatrist for the first time. Maike was there too. I wondered who would show up to that meeting. Would Trish deal with him as she normally dealt with psychiatrists? As it turned out, the others let me deal with the meeting by myself. Again, I had great fear of not being believed. I had come down from Scotland with the label of emotionally unstable personality disorder (borderline) and was worried that this psychiatrist would continue with that diagnosis. But I had another surprise. He said I 'presented with a consistent history of sustained trauma and abuse and a presentation in a number of different personalities'. This pattern, he said, is 'well recognised in victims of sustained traumatic abuse'. Also 'it was unsurprising in some ways that she is finding it difficult to adapt to life away from her abusers'. That 'from time to time unfamiliar emotions and her responses to them had led her to feel quite suicidal and it is clear that she will need substantial on-going support. She is likely to be quite vulnerable and her caution in establishing relationships is sensible and reassuring'. Oh, and he said I made good eye contact!!

It really is quite good that professionals here always write a copy of what was discussed, because I then have an accurate record of what was said. Finally, it seemed that I had both Maike and a psychiatrist who not only believed in DID, but also believed in ritual abuse. This felt good - but it did throw me a bit, because I was used to having my reality denied. It would take time to actually trust their belief. To be listened to and believed makes such a huge difference for people with DID.

In July, Maike got the Crisis Team involved in my case, and I went into respite for a week. My psychiatrist felt that, as the respite house was a small place with only 6 bedrooms, it was more like the Retreat Centre had been, and was therefore a much better option than hospital. I could not have agreed more. However, when I went to meet the team at the respite house, I discovered that they were expecting me to stay for a month. No chance! That was completely out of my comfort zone. I knew that I needed somewhere safe to be for a while, but I stuck my heels in and said that I would stay for a week. The first day I was seriously nervous and didn't know what to do with myself, so I just sat in a chair. Trish was not happy, as she felt that she should have been able to look after us but she couldn't.

The daily routine involved me getting my own breakfast and lunch. Supper was made by the staff and we all ate that meal together. On the second day, Suzie went to the office and said that she was starving. We could not manage breakfast or lunch. Not only was it a big kitchen, but there was too much choice. We kept walking in and out of the kitchen but not managing to get food. The staff were good. They took me into the kitchen to choose a cereal for breakfast. They put my choice of box in a particular place, and told me that, the next morning, all I would have to do would be to get the box, bowl and milk. It worked, as the choice was taken away. Lunch was more difficult but, again, the staff helped. We went into the kitchen and they narrowed the choice so that I could make a decision. Sometimes, if they were making something for themselves, they'd set aside a portion for me. This helped a lot with my food-and-choice issues.

As I get lost in strange places and was feeling quite suicidal, I did not go out on my own. When one of the staff had some spare time, we would go out for a walk and have a coffee.

My cousin Sharon came over one afternoon for coffee and, on the Saturday, Lynn and her husband came and took me out for lunch. Lynn sent me several texts asking if I had made lunch. Sometimes I said yes, to keep her happy, and sometimes I said no. I caught up with some much-needed sleep, and, as the staff had my pills, I could be sure that I was taking them properly. Pills can be a problem. Trish does not like anything except our Valium and is inclined to throw them in the bin rather than take them. Or, other times, we take too many because I don't know if another personality has already taken them.

At the end of my week, I decided that I was going home. They asked if I was ready to go and, although I admitted that I probably wasn't, I had said that I would stay a week - and that was that. I went back to Sharon's in the afternoon ready for dog sitting the following day. I knew in myself that I should have stayed longer, but stubborn is my middle name!

One of the results of being in respite was that I had to start explaining things to Sharon and Lynn. They knew little bits but not a lot. Obviously, they knew that I had mental health problems as I had not been working for most of my life. Now I had to be honest with them. Lynn certainly wanted an explanation. So, over the phone, I explained what life had been like in Scotland, and I explained about having DID. Lynn said that I should have told them years ago, so that my family in England could have done something to get me back in England and keep me safe.

I don't know why I had never told them. Perhaps because of my Dad. I did not want his brothers to think that he was weak. Did I think that he was weak? I'm not sure. He could never stand up to Mother's family. But did that make him weak? Perhaps he was as much under their control as I was. He was the only family member I had a relationship with in Scotland. The only person I ever learned things from was him. If I had told Sharon and Lynn's father what was happening, I have no doubt that he would have done something about it. But would my father have admitted what was happening? Would he ever have forgiven me for sharing what he probably saw as private business? I wonder if my Dad ever had regrets. Did he ever think that he should have taken me and returned to England? These questions are all 'what ifs', and don't really matter, because my life was what it was, and is what it is. No amount of wondering will ever change that.

I think that explaining my condition and its causes to Sharon and Lynn was a positive move, though they both coped with it in different ways. I certainly felt more relaxed in their company, and I did not worry so much about switching. I did get concerned when Lynn that said she had told her daughters, as I was embarrassed. I felt that I would become the family 'crazy person'. But Lynn explained that her daughters would have a better understanding of me if they knew about my condition. So now they have the facts but not the emotions (surprise, surprise). Perhaps they do understand me better now. I wish I understood me better. Sometimes, when I am at Lynn's, she will tell me which of my personalities she has been talking to and fill in any conversations I may have missed. This helps, I guess, as I no longer have gaps. But it is disconcerting that other people know more of what I have been saying than I do.

By August, my psychiatrist had decided that I was 'presenting with symptoms suggesting a significant depressive illness' and wanted to try new pills. I was still impressed that he involved me in discussions as to what medication may or may not work.

In September, Maike made a care plan. This made interesting reading, as it showed that she had a pretty good understanding of me. In the plan she stated that I had difficulties in showing my true emotions, and that this often resulted in me laughing when I was struggling. And there was I thinking that she had not seen through that one! She also noted that, because of my switching, I often needed things written down so I could refer back to them at a later date. It was noted that my dissociation resulted in my not being able to access new activities or social events. Transport was also a problem, because I can get lost when using public transport. Decisions cannot be made quickly as I need time to remember conversations. Also noted was the fact that I need prompting and encouragement when it comes to food. To maintain my independence around food, she suggested some aids, like alarm clocks, or a reduced choice of food items. I guess it was no surprise that she noted I had issues around feeling safe and trusting people. It was decided that she would put in an application for a care package giving me access to respite care four times a year and a personal assistant for 8 hours a week. Unfortunately, it took about 8 months to get this funding in place. I was also on a waiting list for psychotherapy which, again, would take some time due to the waiting lists.

By September, my relationship with professionals was being put to the test. I was advised to stop driving for a while until things settled. The whole issue of whether I could drive or not was only settled 11 months later. Initially, Maike suggested that I stop for a few weeks, which I did. I was not happy, though, as it meant that Sharon had to come and pick me up every week when I went to dog sit. That made me feel like a child. I also felt that, if I had to take buses everywhere, I was more at risk. In my car I felt safe, and the car gave me independence. Maike said that when I came back from a visit to Scotland at the end of September we would discuss it again. However, it began to drag on. My patience wore thin. More truthfully, my patience ran out and I started to drive into Sharon's on a Wednesday and home again on a Thursday. I felt that the whole situation was stupid, as I had driven all my life and never once had an accident. How many people can say that? My psychiatrist said that I should inform the DVLA of my condition. I chose to ignore him. He sent a sheet to me via Maike highlighting that I had a personality disorder and depression and should not be driving. As DID is not a personality disorder, and as I did not have severe depression, I did not in fact have a notifiable condition so far as the DVLA were concerned. I think that the whole issue could have been handled far more easily if my psychiatrist had been talking to me rather than sending messages through Maike. The whole subject of driving became 'the elephant in the room' every time Maike came to visit. Every time I looked out my window and saw the car I got stressed, Trish got furious, and Suzie got upset. It seriously felt like people were trying to control me, and I had suffered all my life with being controlled. I was taking it really badly.

Throughout 2016, I was becoming more and more stressed. Memories and emotions were surfacing. The driving issue was really beginning to get to me. The delay in getting a care package was frustrating. But these were almost minor issues in comparison to what began in May.

Joyce started sending me texts every day instead of e-mails. This was an unexpected change, and I began to worry that something was not right. But she would not tell me anything. As usual, if she did not want to answer a question she just ignored it. Just after my first appointment with the psychiatrist she phoned me. She asked if I had found it useful and whether he accepted that I had DID. She asked if I was still getting on okay with Maike and was happy that I had support in place. Then she told me that she had been in hospital for almost ten days.

There followed weeks of worry. She was getting tests done but seemed always to be waiting for results. The uncertainty was agonising. During that time Mary came down for a week's holiday and I think I must have driven her crazy because my stress levels were hitting the roof.

I thought in my heart that Joyce's cancer had returned and she was just not telling me. I asked her this outright in a text and she told me that it was possible, but so long as they could operate she felt that it would be ok. I started to think about how she had been since she retired from the Retreat Centre. I knew that she had not been feeling well and had told me that she was experiencing 'one thing after another'. I had put all this down to a physical reaction to her retirement and her move to England. She had been under a lot of stress for a couple of years at the Retreat Centre, trying to get funding in place and discussing the expansion of the building. But now I felt that there was a lot more to it.

A lot of people did not know that Joyce was in hospital and were worried about her lack of communication. Eventually, I got a phone call from one of the volunteers who used to work with Joyce. She thought that if anyone would know something, it would be me. So, any information I got I would pass on to her, and she would inform all the other deeply concerned people. Joyce had unwittingly invoked a Catch-22. She never wanted to worry people, so was saying very little about what was wrong. But her silence in itself was more worrying than knowledge of her illness would have been. The brain abhors a knowledge-vacuum, and people were imagining all kinds of nightmare scenarios.

Just after Mary went back to Scotland I got a text from Joyce saying that she had the results.

It was cancer and it was inoperable.

She apologised for the shockwaves her text would cause and asked me to text Sarah (the friend I had made in the retreat centre) with the news. I sent Sarah a text asking her to ring me as I felt it was not the kind of news I could convey by text. That was a really hard phone call. Sarah was upset, and so was I, but I was trying to hold myself together to be there for her.

Either that day or the following, I got the news that Joyce had been told she only had about two weeks to live. This awful news had an unexpected and unfamiliar effect upon my previously buried emotions. They all resurfaced, all at once. Going from having very few emotions to having a whole range of very strong emotions was overwhelming.

I rang Maike in tears, I rang Mary in tears. I just could not cope with what felt like utter devastation. I spoke to Sharon and she said that her husband would drive me the 300 miles to see Joyce. Joyce was not sure about that idea but I was so stressed that I told her I was coming anyway.

Joyce's daughter sent me a text which said that Joyce had been sleeping a lot and she did not know if she would be awake to talk to me. She said that Joyce really did want to see me but it felt like an awful long way for me to come for a short time, especially if Joyce would not necessarily be able to engage much with me. I understood this, but at that point I did not care how far it was. I just wanted to see her and say goodbye.

We left early in the morning to go to the hospital, three days after I had got the terrible news. I hate being on motorways under ordinary circumstances, but I was so focused on getting to Joyce that I hardly noticed I was on one.

When I arrived, Joyce's daughter and grandson went to have coffee so that Joyce and I could have time together. It was lovely to finally meet her daughter, but I wish it could have been under different circumstances. I felt so sorry for her daughter, as they had made all sorts of plans for spending time together in Joyce's retirement and now they were not going to get the time.

Joyce and I spoke for about an hour and a half. She spoke about her death, and how she felt that God's timing was terrible. She had wanted to go back to the Retreat Centre for the reopening celebrations after the renovation work, but now she could not do it. She spoke about her funeral. She told me that people wanted a memorial service at the Retreat Centre, but she was not so sure. That was typical, as she never liked a fuss being made over her. I thought that it was a good idea, as a great many people in Scotland would not be able to attend the funeral in England. She asked me about who I thought would be good to organise this memorial service and I came up with a few names. She began to come around to the memorial service idea, and even suggested I go to that rather than to her funeral as she felt the memorial would be more "her" than the funeral. We discussed the possibility of me reading something at the memorial as she felt I would do that well. No pressure there then!

Neither one of us cried. I knew she wouldn't want tears. We just held hands and spoke. I had started writing my story several years before but had stopped for a couple of years. She asked me to promise her to finish it as she thought it was a story that needed telling and would help others. I kept my promise. You have the evidence in your hands.

Leaving Joyce was the most painful thing I have ever done. She really did feel like my surrogate mother and until that day I never realised just how deeply I loved her. I will always remember her final words to me. As I looked at her from the door she said 'you did well'. I wonder what I did well with. Was it because I didn't cry and therefore made it easier for her? Was it that she thought I had done well in moving to England? I think perhaps she felt I had done well in getting so far as I had done.

After I left the hospital we went to a pub, where I drank a couple of glasses of wine in double quick time and we headed home.

I continued to send Joyce texts every day, just telling her that I was thinking of her and sending her love. As usual I went in to Sharon's on the Wednesday evening and did my dog sitting on the Thursday. For weeks her dog had been cuddling up beside me. It's strange how dogs pick up on a person's emotions. I found it rather comforting to have her on my lap. On the Thursday the dog and I went out for our usual walk. I was just about to turn around and head back to Sharon's when a text came in. It was Joyce's daughter saying that Joyce had passed away peacefully at 11pm the night before.

As I was out in public, I tried to hold it together. Looking back, the spectacle the dog and I must have made at that time seems funny now. You see, I was trying to hold it together but the dog just went crazy, jumping around all over the place. Perhaps my distress was distressing her. When we got back to Sharon's I broke down and the dog disappeared into another room. I suspect that she could not cope with the emotion she was picking up from me.

Sara was a great help to me during this time. She had previously said to me that when something happened to Joyce I would take it very badly. At the time I did not believe her but her words proved to be true. We had several phone calls where she acknowledged my feelings and just listened. She reminded me that Joyce would always be with me but in a different way. That all I had learned from her would stay with me and I could draw on that. The relationship may not be there in a physical way, but it would still be there.

It was shortly after Joyce's death on the 22nd June, that I spent the week in Respite. I felt that the combination of memories surfacing, flashbacks, nightmares plus Joyce's death was more than I could safely cope with.

I did not go to the funeral, but I was sent a copy of the service. The memorial service in the Retreat Centre was not until the beginning of October. Mary came down for the week and we were supposed to be travelling to Scotland in her car. My nerves were so shattered that I couldn't do it, and I ended up taking the train.

Mary and I had a few days at Mary's house before travelling further north for the service. We met Sarah and we went together. It felt strange to see the place with its extension. It felt alien with its security door system and locks on all the bedroom doors. Because it had been extended it was now subject to health and safety rules and no longer felt like a welcoming home as it had in the past.

But perhaps the biggest shock was that there was no Joyce.

In a way, I felt that God's timing had perhaps been right. I don't think that Joyce would have liked all the rules. It was, however, a beautiful memorial. The tributes to her were beautiful and I managed to do the reading. Joyce's sister, daughter and grandson were there. Her daughter gave me a huge hug, asking how her surrogate sister was. She gave me one of Joyce's rings that I had always liked plus her guardian angel on a chain. There had been a song called "You Lift Me Up" played at the funeral and I had asked one of the Retreat Centre trustees if they could play it at the memorial. It is a song that can be interpreted in a spiritual way but I listened to it in a personal way as Joyce was the one who lifted so many up. They played it at the end. The trustee said to me afterwards that at the funeral she had found the song uplifting, but at the memorial there was not a dry eye. Perhaps others felt the same way as me – that they had been lifted up by her.

I did not stay very long. I spoke to Joyce's family and a few others but my emotion was too much to handle. I was amazed at how many of the people I spoke to seemed to be aware of my relationship with Joyce, and how close we had been. I was amazed that her daughter did not seem to have a problem with me being like a surrogate daughter.

The three of us left quite early, and went to the B&B we were staying in. The following day Mary took us out for some sightseeing and then she headed home. Sarah and I spent some time just talking about memories, and the following morning we were on the train south, so we both had company until York where she had to change trains. I felt lost, emotionally. I knew that I would never return to the Retreat Centre. Never again sit in the kitchen chatting to Joyce. Never enjoy the amazing views of nature or help out in the garden. Because it looked so different with its extension, this was, in a way, easier than I had expected. But being there made Joyce's death so much more of a reality.

In my usual way, I had thought that the memorial would bring closure. As usual I was wrong. I couldn't open my e-mails for weeks as it was too painful not to find one from her every morning. I struggled with the knowledge that I could no longer talk to her on the phone. If Maike asked me what she could do to help I replied "get Joyce here for an hour". Her absence made me appreciate just what a special person she was. There was nothing I could not say to her.

There was never judgement. Never anger. No matter what state I was in, I had always moved, emotionally, after a conversation with her. She gave me the space to work things out for myself. She never told me what to do. Except for telling me not to talk to a therapist (sorry Joyce, I am seeing one, but it became a necessity!).

I lost the spiritual side of me when Joyce died. Since moving to England I had not found anything spiritual to do. I could have gone to one of the Retreat Centres here but chose not to. I ask myself, was I angry with God (whoever he or she may be) after Joyce died? I don't know. I was upset that she never got to enjoy her retirement with her daughter. I was upset that she had given her life to the Retreat Centre and that the pressures of the last couple of years had taken its toll on her health. I was upset because certain people there wanted her to retire. I don't know the answers. I know that I threw out all my Spiritual Direction books. The only spiritual books I have left are the ones Joyce gave me, but I can't read them. Perhaps I feel the same as Joyce – that God's timing was not good for me either. We had been planning trips to visit each other and it saddened me that she would never see where I lived.

I don't know what happens when someone dies but I still feel Joyce's presence. She is still a big influence on my life. In my worst moments, I feel that I have let her down. This feeling was particularly strong in the months immediately following her death. After her many years of trying to support me I felt that my return to England had not been as successful as Joyce had hoped. I was not functioning any better than I had been in Scotland. I had been into A&E feeling suicidal. I was not able to make a life for myself. I was not sure if I even wanted a life.

Would Joyce really be disappointed with me, though, or do I just think she would be? I am here, safe and alive so perhaps that alone would please her. Perhaps it is me that is disappointed with me.

Chapter 11

Recovery is not a straight line

I think it became obvious to me in 2016 that recovery does not happen in a straight line. It is not a case of tough but steady progress. There are ups and downs, steps back as well as forward. There are many times when I want to give up, and also times when I find the strength to keep going. Sometimes I find that I have been moving forward but didn't notice the movement until I look back.

One of the biggest shifts during this phase of my life was that I began for the first time to trust professionals. I realised that I could not recover without help and support. It wasn't easy though, given my previous experiences with mental health professionals.

Having DID can complicate all relationships and this includes relationships with professionals. If one personality does not trust, they can go out of their way to ruin therapeutic relations. Thankfully that has not happened this time, and we all seem to be in agreement that we need help. It's not easy for Maike to cope with having conversations with 3 of us but she seems to be able to go with the flow. One minute she can be chattering to a seven-year-old, and the next a 29-year-old will be swearing her head off at her. And there are also the other four personalities who are beginning to communicate. Maike gives us all the space to express ourselves, which is so important. They are all aspects of me, and we need to be able to say what is important to each one of us. Without all of us being able to talk about our experiences, I feel that healing will never happen.

One of the most important things about Maike is that we trust her physically. Because I have been abused so much, and some of that abuse has come from professionals, I am very wary. But I can sit next to Maike on my sofa and have no fear of anything abusive happening. This feeling of physical safety allows me to verbally open up to her. I do have moments of fear. I get afraid that, by talking to her, I am showing her my vulnerability, and that as a result she will hurt me. But I am learning to recognise that my fear is being caused by the past and not because of anything in my relationship with her.

I also began to be less silent about having mental health problems. Trish enjoys having a drink in the local pub a couple of times a week. Sometimes this is just because she enjoys a drink, but sometimes she heads pubwards because it is her way of coping with emotion.

I also enjoy having a drink. But being out in the local pub can cause problems. I don't remember conversations and I don't remember the times that Trish has been there. So, some days I can find myself struggling to continue a conversation that I have no memory of ever participating in. But I have ways of covering up problematic moments. Trish and I can sound pretty much the same – except when she is angry - so to lots of people it is not so obvious that I am not me.

One day I was upset over the driving issue and went to the pub without realising that I had red eyes from the effort of not crying. The landlady came to check that I was ok and I ended up just letting a lot of stuff out. Though I found it embarrassing, it actually worked out for the best. I felt safer being there because I had been honest. I also discovered that if I am honest with people then people end up being honest with me. Quite often people will tell me about problems in their lives. I don't shout it from the roof tops that I have mental health problems. Not everyone would understand. But if the landlord and landlady, plus a few of the staff know about my situation then I don't feel so vulnerable in the pub.

This was also the year that Trish started to struggle with her role as protector. Each personality has a role to fulfil and hers was to protect us. She is also the one who stands between Suzie and me and the other four personalities who hold the worst memories of abuse. I don't know why she began to struggle. Perhaps she had been too strong for too long. She began to trust Maike, inasmuch as she trusts anyone (not much!). But Trish's burgeoning relationship with Maike was not always plain sailing. One time, she backed Maike into a corner. We were not in a good place emotionally and Maike wanted to ring the Crisis Team. I find the Crisis Team difficult, as you always get a different person. Some of them understand a bit about DID but most of them don't. The Crisis Team suggestion made Suzie and I afraid, and Trish hit the roof with anger.

It must be hard for Maike sometimes to decide if we are safe or not, but she is good at risk-management. I have learned that if we all talk to her about what the problem is we can usually find a way to cope and get through any crisis.

I still found it hard to express emotions at this point. Still do, if I am honest! I often want to burst into tears or scream my head off that I can't cope. But even now I rarely do – and I definitely did not back then! I think there may have been a couple of times when I cried a little with Maike, but it has always been second nature for me to fight tears. However, I was getting better at talking about what I felt. Admitting to my problems with everyday living. Admitting fear or confusion. Admitting to suicidal feelings.

Feelings of suicide can be difficult for someone with DID and difficult for the professionals or friends who are supporting them. Many studies have shown that we have one of highest suicide rates and are considered a very 'at risk' group.

Having said this, it is very difficult to accurately assess a person with DID's suicide risk at any one time because many personalities are involved. One personality may be feeling suicidal while the others are not. Or another personality may be feeling suicidal but I am not aware of it. As can be imagined this can get complicated. Another personality may make a suicide attempt without me being aware of it. On a few occasions I have been taken to A&E feeling suicidal, only for another personality to take over and present no signs of being suicidal whatsoever.

It's also worth noting that some personalities do not realise that by killing themselves they are killing all of us, because they see themselves as being totally separate entities. These personalities can cause a lot of harm to our body, thinking that they are the only ones who will have to bear the brunt of the consequences. But, of course, their behaviour hurts us all. So, you see, the risks for people with DID are horribly real.

Though I found the death of Joyce devastating, it also had a healing aspect. But that realization only came recently.

Joyce's devastating death was actually the day I emotionally 'joined the human race'. Instead of being able to block out the terrible grief in my usual manner, I swung to the opposite extreme. I had felt emotion before, but I had always managed to get it under control pretty quickly and pack it away in a box in my mind. When Joyce died, it was impossible to box the emotion I felt away. Nor did I want to. It felt as though to denying the pain would be to deny Joyce and all she had done for me. I had loved Joyce, and I had trusted her, so I had to carry on trusting the emotions she released in me. I had to allow myself to feel the pain of her loss.

But this emotional release came at a bad time. Joyce's death coincided with the controversy over whether or not I should be driving, and the delay in the care package. Suddenly there was emotion everywhere. Trish would look out the window at the car and go into a fury she could hardly contain. She saw the injunction on driving as a limitation of her freedom and independence. It felt, for her, as though she was being controlled – and that triggered memories from the past.

I also felt a loss of independence and that also triggered memories. Suzie was full of fear, as when we drove she felt safer and did not get lost. To a lot of people, it may have seemed I was overreacting to the driving thing, but it sparked off so many issues for all of us that it became overwhelming. It was constantly on my mind. But although I could not control the emotions it brought out, at least I was beginning to understand what was happening inside me.

If you've been carefully curtailing your emotions for years, barely experiencing anything like true emotion, you're not at all prepared for the strength of any emotion at all which gets through your barriers. So, to go from my previous emotionally void state to this tidal wave of grief, frustration, and rage was overwhelmingly difficult. It's something I'm still working on. A work in progress.

Chapter 12

Potholes in Recovery Road

The beginning of 2017 started in a bad way and, frankly, it continued to be a hard year. Many of the problems I was facing coalesced around the driving issue – which brought me head to head with Maike in a way which both Trish and I found very difficult.

Mid way through January Maike said she thought I could drive so I went out to celebrate by buying curtains etc. for my flat. Two days later, Maike rang me to say that my psychiatrist had different ideas and thought I should not be driving. This was followed by a further call from Maike saying that the psychiatrist had issued a warning – if I did not inform the DVLA of my condition, then he would. I still held the view that DID was not on the list of notifiable conditions for the DVLA and felt like control of my life was being taken out of my hands. Again.

When Maike phoned me with this news I simply hung up the phone in a state of shock and frustration. I went to the pub, to try and calm myself down – to no avail. I felt that I could no longer cope with everything being up in the air. The driving licence problem, the care package not being set up and everything else that was going around in my head just got too much.

These mixed messages were the final straw. Later that day I found myself once again off to A&E in an ambulance, courtesy of Maike, who phoned the emergency services out of concern for my safety. I was, admittedly, feeling pretty suicidal. When the hospital asked me what had happened I just told them "my care manager and psychiatrist happened". The hospital teams did their usual assessments. As usual though "my eye contact was good and I had a sense of humour". Even I was getting fed up with my defence system but I couldn't show my true feelings.

The driving problem had been around for months and because it was Maike who told me, I felt that my hard-won trust in her was completely gone. At the hospital they asked if it would have been better if the psychiatrist had given me the driving news. Of course, it would have been, as I did not have a trusting relationship with him. I had only seen him a few times and though I liked him I did not trust him as such.

Maike and I struggled with the issue of trust for quite a while after that. I felt that I could not talk to her in the same way as before. She asked me if I wanted to get rid of her and have someone else. But I felt that I would not trust anyone new either, so we tried to work it out between us.

People who have been abused have huge problems trusting others. With me, if trust is broken then I will not try to rebuild it. Trust, to me, was a hard-won, sacred thing, which lost its sanctity and became worthless if violated.

So now I had a problem. I had trusted Maike as much as I could, and it felt as though she had violated that trust. I wanted to tell her, and all the professionals, to go to hell. But I also realised that I needed help and support. It was a real dilemma. Should I try to rebuild the trust, or cope on my own?

'Coping on my own' had never worked out well for me in the past. With my increasingly clear perspective on my life, I saw that it was similarly unlikely to work this time, either. So, I had to go against my own instincts regarding trust, turn my back on my self-imposed trust-taboos, and try to rebuild the broken trust between Maike and I.

This was (and still is) seriously hard work, let me assure you. I managed to regain a certain level of trust with Maike after a while, but it did not feel the same. I felt wary of what I said to her for many, many months after that day. It took a long, long time to get back to where we had been, with plenty of slip ups.

But I managed eventually. This may not seem like such a big deal but, for me, that felt like huge progress. Not only had I rebuilt valuable trust with someone important to me, but I had also rewritten the relational patterns of my own life. That's nearly impossible for a neurotypical person to do, let alone someone like me! I felt proud of myself. But it took a lot of difficulty and turmoil to start me on that journey in the first place.

In the meantime, the driving issue was not going away. I asked for an appointment with the psychiatrist and saw him at the end of January. I felt that if he was making all these decisions about my driving then the least he could do was talk to me, and not keep sending messages via Maike. Maike was going to come with me but ended up being off sick that day. So, I put on my calm, cool and collected face and went to see him.

By the end of the conversation, he said that there was no longer any reason for him to insist I did not drive, but he had to talk to his colleagues about it. His colleagues however unanimously decided that I should contact the DVLA so they could have clarity about the situation in the future. Again, I felt as though I was being controlled by nameless, faceless people. I filled in the form and notified the DVLA in February and was led to believe they would take six weeks to make their decision. They eventually made their decision in August – six months, to save you counting up on your fingers! Their decision after all that time was to send me for a medical examination. Maybe they were hoping to find something medically wrong with me because they could not make up their minds about DID. Certainly, that is what the doctor I saw thought. Unfortunately for them, I was fine physically. So, after months of needless stress and anxiety I got a medical licence valid for a year, to be reviewed every year. Better than nothing, but I was still angry.

I decided to go to Scotland to visit Mary towards the end of March. Waiting for the DVLA decision was agonising, and I was stressing every time the mail arrived. It would be easier, I felt, to be away for a while.

Unfortunately, that was not one of my better decisions.

I had felt nervous about getting on the train, which was unusual for me. Just over an hour into the journey the train driver slammed on the brakes and under my carriage there was a horrible noise. The other passengers said it sounded like we had gone over a large branch but in my mind, it was not a branch, it was a person. Turned out, to my horror, that I was right.

I couldn't get that noise out of my head. Nor could I stop thinking about who that person had been. Troublingly, I also began thinking that jumping under a train was a good way of dying. I thought it was a better than an overdose.

In Scotland, that horrible noise would not get out of my head. It joined with other memories to form an unpleasant mental trip into my past. I went to visit Derek and Janet but my mind was constantly flooded with memories of things that had happened up there. The day I saw Janet and Derek was exactly 16 years since I had moved in with them. That brought back the memory of why I had moved in with them in the first place. A memory of horrendous abuse. It felt like all the locked boxes in my mind were beginning to fly open. In a sense, I could see myself running around in my mind, pushing memories back into their boxes. As soon as I got one lid back on, another lid would fly open.

I felt traumatised by what had happened on the train but could not understand why. My usual response would have been not to give it a second thought -which I appreciate sounds callous, but (as I have said) blocking out painful emotions was my old way of dealing with them. Now, though, it felt like I was actually over-reacting. I was feeling traumatised – and not only by what had happened to that poor person under the train, but also by the memories which were surfacing unbidden as I visited my Scottish friends.

The fact that I was feeling emotion was overwhelming. But the difficult part was that I couldn't let the emotions out. They were stuck inside me. On the outside I looked fine but inside I was falling apart.

When I came back from Scotland I met a man in my local pub one evening. I had never met him before and we started chatting. I thought it would be like talking to other people I knew there but it wasn't. He asked me to go to the other pub in the village with him. I didn't want to but couldn't say no. Afterwards he walked me home holding my hand which totally freaked me out on the inside. But, again, I could do nothing about it on the outside. When we got to my door he said he would have come in but he was too drunk. Only when I got into my flat did I start shaking. I knew I could not have said no to him had he wanted to come up. Again, the issue of not being able to 'no' had come back to haunt me. I think that this problem is common for people from my background, who have been conditioned into acquiescence.

The next time I was in the pub I spoke to the landlady and explained the problem. The next time the guy came into the pub I went out through the back door so it did not happen again. The landlady explained to the staff to make sure I did not leave the pub with a man. That made me feel safer, but I was frustrated that I could not find it in myself to say no.

After being told to give people what they want all my life, it is really difficult to learn that I have choices. This inability affects all my relationships. I constantly feel the need to please people because I am afraid of their reaction if I don't. The strange thing is that I don't feel that way with Maike. I can say no to her and disagree with what she says. Sometimes it feels like I can practice things with her. It's because I don't fear her reaction. I know that she will not hurt me physically, emotionally or sexually. I trust that she will hold her professional boundaries and therefore I feel safe. Not all professionals are like that though and I have been with professionals who have overstepped the mark in emotional and sexual ways. I don't know what makes her different. Perhaps her honesty and openness. Perhaps because she accepts us all. Perhaps because her desire to help me does not come with an agenda. Perhaps because I do not feel that I have to please her in anyway at all.

By June, I was really struggling. I was going to a group on Tuesday morning in the next town where we played pool, table tennis, chatted. When I left the flat that particular morning I knew that after the group I was not going home. My mind was on train tracks.

One of the support workers went to a café for coffee with me and phoned Maike as she was concerned about what I was saying. Maike said that she would ring me in a couple of hours. However, I couldn't stay in my flat waiting for her to ring. I put my mobile off and headed for the train line. When I was almost there I suddenly heard Suzie screaming "no" inside my head. That scream stopped me right there and then. I stood there, my train of thought (please excuse the grim pun) derailed. I switched my mobile on to discover messages from Maike. I texted her and said where I was. She said to phone her when I got home.

When I made my way home, I found four policemen standing in my flat. Maike had put out alerts. Yet another trip to A&E, this time chauffeured in a police car. I guess the eye contact and humour were still working well as I got home after the usual talking routine.

In July Mary came down for a week's holiday and I felt safe having her around. We went out and about which was nice. With DID, I don't get out much. It's too easy for me to get lost and end up somewhere I don't know. Plus, I feel too vulnerable as I can easily be triggered.

As I have four personalities who have never lived in the world they are very vulnerable to the sexual advances of someone. If I am triggered by something and switch into one of them then there can be dangerous consequences. I can have evidence later of rough sex having happened but have no memory of it. I think Maike has had some communication with a couple of them, but they won't say to her what is happening in their lives. Or rather, they are not saying enough to enable Maike to do anything to protect them.

In September 2017 I wondered if it was possible to have a nervous breakdown quietly. An unseen breakdown. Breakdown or not, I ended up in respite care, during which time I did a lot of reflection.

After a week I came home. Maike had suggested that I stay a bit longer but as usual my stubbornness won the day. Even on the short journey home I knew I had made a mistake and should have stayed longer. But I was feeling so bad that I knew that staying a short while longer would not helped me to feel better. The problems were still there in respite and they would still be there when I got home.

Chapter 13

Therapy – The Rocky Process of Self-Discovery

My thoughts on therapy are mixed, and very dependent upon the individual therapist.

Therapists and care managers obviously have trained and have the certificates to prove it. They have listened to lectures and read books. My guess is that not too many training courses in the NHS spend much, if any, time on DID. Those professionals who do understand DID are the ones who have gone out there and researched the subject themselves with an open mind. Some professionals think that switching personalities is something that is caused by stress. If we switch we are stressed and if we don't then we are reasonably stable. I would disagree with that. Yes, sometimes something will happen when I feel stressed and Trish will take over but lots of the time we switch because another personality just wants to do something or say something. For me the amount of times I switch is not really the most important issue. What is important is for me to find a way to stop the internal conflict between us. To share our memories with each other, learn how to live in harmony with each and develop loving relationships between us all.

For me, it is not the number of certificates a professional has that really matters. Yes, they need the knowledge to be able to help us but what is really important is 'who they are'. For me, it is only human love that can help me recover. My life has been largely one of abuse, hurt and rejection. The only way I can heal is to experience being truly cared for. In experiencing this care, I can learn how to care for myself.

Many professionals do not think that a client should rely on them and therefore keep a professional distance. I think that people with DID need to be able to rely on their professional team. We need to feel safe enough to explore the pain inside ourselves. If some professional sits with us with their 'professional' mask on we are not going to be able to trust. Our abusers wore masks and we never knew where we were with them. Our relationship and trust issues are based on our past experiences. In order to heal we need to experience safe, contained, caring and trusting relationships. Relationships where we feel our physical boundaries are not going to be violated as they were in the past.

The added complication with having DID is that professionals have to build relationships with all of us. It's a bit like doing family therapy. They have to build safe and trusting relationships with all of us which is easier said than done. I have been told that all the parts of me are really just me. The part that holds the anger, the part that is the childlike part of me. For me that feels really insulting. I know that Suzie and Trish find it insulting. We share the same body but we are separate and unique people. It feels invalidating to be told they are just a part and not a person. We have had too much invalidation in our lives. If they are told they are just parts then they will not trust enough to open up and talk.

Once we have learned within our therapeutic relationships that we can trust, feel cared for and begin to love ourselves we develop the confidence to try these skills out in the outside world. It's a bit like the analogy of the caterpillar. Eventually we can develop the wings we need to fly.

Just before my March trip to Scotland, I had begun Cognitive Analytical Therapy. The name of my therapist reminds me of someone in Scotland who I associate with bad memories. So, to get around that problem I mentally call her CAT Woman.

She explained to me that there are three stages involved in trauma therapy. The first stage is to ''establish safety and stabilization". This includes bodily safety, safe environment and emotional stability. Once I was 'safe' in the here and now then I could remember the trauma rather than reliving it. The second stage is "coming to terms with the memories". Just remembering the trauma does not bring about recovery. The goal is to come to terms with my traumatic past. The third stage is "integration and moving on". The aim is to have a healthy present and a healed self. The idea being that I will ultimately be able to form healthy attachments and attain personal goals.

She showed me a sheet which explained what trauma did to a person and their way of thinking. I listed these symptoms previously but they are worth listing again here. They include

- Loss of sense of 'who I am'
- Self-destructive behaviour
- Feeling unreal or out of my body
- Substance abuse or eating disorders
- Chronic pain, headaches,
- General anxiety and panic attacks
- Hypervigilance and Mistrust
- Nightmares and flashbacks
- Few or no memories
- Shame and worthlessness

- Hopelessness
- Loss of a sense of the future
- Emotional overwhelm
- Insomnia
- Lack of concentration
- Feeling of numbness
- Apathy
- Depression and irritability.

She explained that after trauma a person is always prepared for danger. This shows itself in two ways. I either have hyperarousal or hypo arousal. Hyper means I get emotionally overwhelmed, overly vigilant, panicking, angry and have racing thoughts. When hypo I feel like I have no feelings. I feel numb, shut down and as though I am not really here.

I am seldom in a mental place where my feelings and reactions are tolerable. This causes problems with attachment. I swing between the two extremes. I feel it's not safe to be connected and not safe to trust. But on the other hand, I want to be connected because I don't want to be alone. I get confused as to whether I want to run away from people or run towards them. Some days I feel numb and flat. Others I feel out of control. Or I may be having lots of flashbacks or nightmares. I can feel painful body sensations as though the abuse is still happening. When overwhelmed by all of this I am not able to cope with normal everyday life. I don't feel safe in the world or inside my own skin.

Learning all of this was like being hit over the head with a brick. I knew that my emotions in the last two years had being breaking through but to read about it in this way was frightening to say the least.

No one had ever shown me that trauma had all those effects and I was shocked to discover that I had them all. Plus, I had Dissociative Identity Disorder. I did not exactly leave my first therapy session full of hope. I had been told we would have 20 sessions of one hour a week and, frankly, I did not see how all those stages were going to be worked though in 20 hours. The sessions have now been increased to 60 but, as I am now at about session 47 and really don't feel I have succeeded in completing stage one I think I need a miracle in the next 10 weeks!

I think people need to be aware that doing therapy requires a fine balancing of risk with safety. I have heard people say that therapy can make you feel worse before you feel better. I wholeheartedly agree with this. The past can't be resolved without having old memories reactivated or new memories being shared between personalities. There needs to be safety around doing this because if we are overwhelmed by feelings of unsafety we are just repeating patterns of the past and not resolving anything. I think there is a real danger with DID patients that when therapy ends they are left in a worse state than they before. A negative thought, perhaps, but I believe it's a valid concern.

The first thing my therapist and I looked at was "appreciating my strengths". When it comes to looking at my survival and creative resources I discovered a problem. I was brought up feeling unloved, rejected, controlled and worthless. As a result, I see myself as inadequate, incompetent, unworthy and full of shame and guilt. This leaves me feeling that I do not have the resources to deal with life. I am very self-critical of my lack of progress and tend to see only my short comings and not my strengths.

But having DID is strength. My other personalities saved me from a lot of the pain. By not crying or showing fear I saved myself from more pain. Trish used anger to push people away and in doing so helped to protect those of us who were vulnerable. Being emotionally withdrawn was a survival response. Being punished for expressing how I felt meant that being emotionally withdrawn protected me. Self-harm could be seen as a survival resource. It was a way of allowing me to feel and get some relief from my inner pain. Even suicidal thoughts gave me some sense of control, which was lacking in the rest of my life.

After thinking about it a lot I realised there were numerous resources I used to cope with the trauma. The easiest way is to list them.

- I "read" other people in an attempt to predict what they will do
- I please other people instead of myself
- I dissociate
- I shut down and become numb
- I comply and submit
- I show only the parts of myself that think others will find acceptable.
- I am hypervigilant
- I experience hyper/hypo arousal
- I flee, run, freeze or hide
- I get angry easily
- I isolate or withdraw.
- I disconnect from myself
- I stop feeling
- I keep emotions that were not accepted under wraps
- I detach from life
- I become apathetic or inactive

- I self-harm
- I under eat
- I drink too much

It was a shock to discover that I was still using many of these techniques even though the abuse had stopped and I was in a safe place.

I began to look at my creative resources. I was quite proud of myself when I managed to find one creative resource. Being in nature and gardening was very important when I lived with Janet and Derek. Now I started to look at being in nature in a more in-depth manner. I asked myself questions about how it felt. Did I find it energizing or calming? Both. Did my breathing change? Yes, it slowed down and became deeper. Was my body more relaxed? Yes, it felt less tense and I felt more grounded. Did the experience make me want to smile? Yes. How did my posture change? I felt that my body was more relaxed. I am still trying to find other creative resources that I can use.

The next topic discussed was Basic Distress Tolerance Skills. Everyone has to cope with distress and pain at some point in their life. I learned in therapy that I cope with emotional pain and physical pain in unhealthy ways. No surprise there then! I tend not to think rationally and therefore can't think of good solutions. I can overthink, get very anxious, isolate myself, feel suicidal or want to self-harm. My self-esteem disappears (is it ever there?) and I feel unworthy of happiness. Basically, I don't (didn't?) have many healthy distress tolerance skills.

What I had to do was to learn to distract myself, relax and cope. Sounds easy, but it is a huge struggle. To distract myself does not mean avoiding the distress. I have, after all, spent all my life avoiding emotions, and it hasn't been a good tactic. Instead, I need to acknowledge the distress but to distract myself so that I can calm down. Once I am calm, and my emotions are at a more tolerable level, I can deal with the distress.

I read about different ways of distracting myself when I felt overwhelming distress. Reading about them and doing them successfully are two completely different things. If I felt like cutting my wrist, one of the suggestions was to draw with a red pen on my wrist where I would usually cut and mark the stitches with a black pen. Definitely did not see this one working for me. Another suggestion was to cry. Again, this would not work as I seldom cry and cannot force myself into it. Snapping a rubber band on my wrist was another non-starter. I did find a couple that appealed to my humour and would be worth a try. My favourite was to draw the faces of people I hated on balloons then pop them. I would need a lot of balloons! Another was to write letters to the people who hurt me and then burn them. But there are so many people who hurt me that it would take forever. Throwing foam balls against a wall sounded helpful, though I would prefer to throw bricks through windows! Foam ball throwing does not have the same sense of satisfaction. I guess that everyone has to find what works for them.

I worked with my therapist on distracting myself with pleasurable activities. She gave me a long list of pleasurable activities but, to be honest, I was hard pushed to find many things on it that I found pleasurable. I also discovered that my personalities found different activities pleasurable. Some of them were just plain stupid for someone with DID. For example, going on a trip to somewhere I have never been before is about the craziest thing I could do. New places stress me, I dissociate and get lost. Or organising a party, which would completely freak me out.

Even when I did find activities I liked they were usually really difficult or impossible to do. When I am distressed I find trying to distract myself almost impossible. Trish tends to distract herself by going to the pub. That, however, was not on the list! On a serious note a lot of the pleasurable activities involved going out and joining groups. This is something I do not deal with as groups stress me. I switch personality and it becomes anything but pleasurable.

We then spoke about distracting my thoughts. Forcing myself to forget about something that happened to me in the past is really difficult. And a person can't simply force themselves to get rid of emotions they find distressing.

However, something needed to be done, no matter how difficult I found it. In the last two years memories and emotions had been coming out at an alarming rate. I needed to try and find a distraction technique that worked for me.

It is easy to see my past as all negative but there were positives I could try to bring to mind. For example, I could remember the good times with Joyce, Sara, Mary, Janet and Derek. I could also remember how much I had enjoyed gardening 2 days a week. I had a book of meditation verses that Joyce had used at the Retreat Centre. These were all things I could use to distract my thoughts from the overwhelming ones. I could also imagine myself having a conversation with Joyce. I knew her so well I could imagine what her responses would be.

Distracting myself by counting is quite good. I try to sit down in a comfortable position and count my breaths, trying to be aware of each inhale and exhale. It is possible to count just about anything. One day I was sitting in my cousin's car waiting for her to collect a prescription. I was aware of my increasing stress so started counting the flowers on the bush in front of me. It may sound stupid but it worked.

Once my therapist and I had spoken about the distraction ideas we moved on to the 'relax' part of 'distract, relax and cope'. If my body feels relaxed, I feel better. I knew that to be true from the healing sessions that Sara used to give me. Many times, I wished that she were closer so I could experience them again. For the period of the healing session I was not in flee/fight/freeze mode. It felt relaxing and my body felt like it belonged to me. I felt more like a connected whole.

I was told that soothing and relaxation could involve all the senses of smell, sight, hearing, taste and touch. Again, it is trying to find what works for me. Being in nature is good as I can try to concentrate on the smell of flowers, newly cut grass, and the smell of the sea. Soothing by the sense of sight again involves nature. I love walking in the woods, surrounded by trees. Or standing on the top of a hill looking out over the countryside. Again, using my sense of hearing involves nature. Listening to the sound of the wind, the sea, a stream, the call of the birds. Music is important to me and I find it soothing. Different music for different moods.

It is impossible for Trish and I to use taste as self-soothing. Well, perhaps that's not totally true. Trish finds the taste of lager very soothing...but doubtless my therapist would not see that as helpful. As Trish never eats there is no food she finds soothing. Quite the opposite, as food triggers memories for her. Suzie, on the other hand, finds chocolate milk, chocolate, lollipops, cakes, ice cream and pudding very soothing. The only problem is that Trish and I tend to forget to buy them for her.

With the sense of touch, I think that our small teddy bear is soothing. Even Trish is coming around to realising that just holding the bear is soothing. Things like long hot showers or baths do not work as water is a trigger. Getting a massage is no good. Touch by a stranger is terrifying. Using body oil or lotion is something I can't do because at the moment I have not learned to love my own body. Though I find water hard to contend with I do love being in my cousin's hot tub. I love the movement of the bubbles and find it really relaxing. I don't think I could actually be in a hot tub alone though.

Before I had managed to get my head round the previous skills my therapist moved me onto advanced distress tolerance skills. How can a therapist expect me to learn a set of skills in a week and be able to take on another chapter? I know therapists have to work within a time frame but I think survivors of extreme, long term abuse cannot recover within this time frame. Plus, I don't believe that therapy is the answer to everything anyway.

But, ready or not, we embarked on the advanced skills. As I was bomb-barded with all this new information I felt a bit like the Titanic heading for the iceberg. We started doing a safe place visualisation. By closing my eyes, I could imagine somewhere where I had felt safe, and by doing so my stress levels would drop. I tried this with my therapist and she asked questions about where I was and what I was seeing. I imagined myself at the Retreat Centre and described to her the mountains, the birds on the bird feeder, the water in front of me and the red squirrels. All went well until she asked me where Joyce was. Was she inside the house or in the garden? My immediate response was "she is not there, she is dead". End of feeling relaxed!

There is also something called cue-controlled relaxation. A cue is a trigger word that helps you to relax. Again, this concept caused problems. People with DID and PTSD are easily triggered by words, smells, taste, etc. The thought of choosing a trigger word, albeit a positive one, was not something I could cope with.

Another suggestion was to try living in the present moment. I know that it is easy for me to live in the past. It is incredibly difficult to escape the past when I am getting flashbacks and memories surfacing. Plus, I have a lot of anger inside about what happened to me in Scotland. Though I am hundreds of miles away, it is an almost constant in my mind and will be there until the issues are resolved.

I think a lot about the future, too. To try and live in the present moment is a constant struggle. I used to be able to do it at the Retreat Centre and during healing sessions with Sara. I find it hard now, though. Perhaps this is because my emotions are now very much at the surface and the memories are overwhelming. The present moment always feels terrible but that is because I am not actually in the present moment. One of the few times I am in the present is when Maike comes to visit. Sometimes I get angry with her, or afraid of her. But looking back I can realise that it is not her I'm afraid of or angry with. It is a reaction that comes from the past. But by talking to Maike when it happens I can understand what is happening, and why. I feel like a bit of a time traveller really. Bouncing from the past and then into the future regularly causes a lot of unnecessary pain. I think I could be in the present moment with Joyce and Sara because they both held a safe and supported space.

I find it almost impossible to feel that my home is a safe space so I always feel stressed there. My mind shoots off in all directions. If I try to stop time travelling and be aware of the present moment I get stuck with the thought that the present moment is not a good moment. Perhaps I am still pretty useless at practicing the distress tolerance skills. Or perhaps I just need some more time to learn them. Rome was not built in a day after all. And I can't expect miracles after just 47 sessions of therapy.

Trying to stay in the present moment by using breathing is sometimes easier. I can concentrate on trying to breathe more deeply and slowly. I learned how to do this with Joyce so I know that I am capable of doing it. At the Retreat Centre I could go to meditation for half an hour and was aware of nothing but my breathing. We spoke about self-encouraging thoughts that I could use to try and lesson my distress. Lots of them were just not helpful. For example, "this too will pass", or "these are just my feelings, they will eventually go away". All they did was make me angry, not encouraged. I had to try and find some that would work for me. Again, my different personalities had different ideas. For me it was, "keep smiling, you can do this". For Trish it is "those bastards in Scotland are not going to crack me up". For Suzie it was "me and my bear are okay".

The next thing my therapist threw at me was the concept of "radical acceptance". This involves looking at myself and the world in different ways. I was led to believe that radically accepting the present moment meant acknowledging the part I played in my current situation. This may work in some situations but for people with DID it felt counterproductive. People who have been abused fight with the thought that the abuse was their fault, that they did something to deserve it. They feel guilt and shame because they feel they were to blame. It takes years to break free from those thoughts. I am now at the point that I know it was not my fault. So, acknowledging the part I played in my situation frankly sounds like an insult.

The Serenity Prayer strikes more a chord with me. It says "grant me the serenity to accept the things I cannot change, courage to change the things I can, and the wisdom to know the difference". This is more in line with my philosophy. Having said this, however, accepting the things I cannot change means accepting the past. While I can accept that the abuse happened and I can't change that, I still feel enough anger to want to see these people face justice. I can't see how I can feel otherwise. To forgive my abusers is something that just is never going to happen. I have great admiration for people who can forgive but I am not one of them. A large part of me wants revenge, which is not a very loving attitude. Given what happened in Scotland with the police and mental health services, legal justice is not an option. Even if it was, I don't have the emotional energy for that route.

So, my revenge has to be my recovery. At least that is showing love towards myself.

Writing this book is also a form of revenge. I want others in my position to see that it is possible to survive. Possible to make a life. But I am not sugar coating it. Recovery is one of the hardest things you will ever do and the desire to give up will live with you daily. One step forward and two back almost becomes the norm.

Continuing the process of therapy, we talked about internal and external resources. Internal resources include being able to talk about feelings, feel bodily sensations, talking easily with other people, being able to set boundaries and being able to reflect on my behaviours. External resources are things like family, friends, clubs, professionals etc.

We made a chart detailing my external resources. They included my cousins, as well as Mary, Sarah, and Sara. Although the last three lived miles away from me, I still had ongoing relationships with them. On the professional side I had Maike, my PA, my therapist, and a support worker I saw at the group I attended on Tuesdays. Also included, but on the edge of my support chart, were my psychiatrist and my GP. To be able to use the support of these people involved being trusting enough to accept this support. It also involved my being able to accept that I deserved the support.

I find it hard to believe that I deserve support because a large part of me thinks I am worthless. The lack of support I had in Scotland has made it difficult for me to believe that there are really are people here in England who want to help. Plus, it is still hard to ask for help as it makes me feel vulnerable and open to rejection. However, I am learning that to be able to recover I do need support. At the end of the day it is only me who can turn my life around but having support as I do so is necessary.

Having these external resources has an effect on my inner being. I began to see that I was worthy of support. That people saw me as likeable and enjoyed my company. I also came to see that people could talk to me about their problems, too. Joyce had often told me that I allowed people the space to talk about themselves and, particularly when I was in the pub, I found this to be true.

Those internal resources, which involved being able to connect with my body and feeling grounded, were much more difficult. Also included in this group was the ability to breathe deeply, have good posture, enjoyment of sexual or sensual activities, and good health. As I mentioned before, the only time I feel connected to my body is when I am in my cousin's hot tub. This means I seldom feel grounded, and my breathing is usually quite shallow.

Though I am fortunate in having good health I do not lead a healthy lifestyle. Because of the issues around food my diet is not good. Because I can't get outdoors on my own I do not get nearly enough physical exercise (unless you call a three-minute walk to the pub exercise). Other than walking to the pub I go for a walk with my cousin and her dog usually once a week. I am deeply aware that I am not getting enough exercise as it feels like my body is getting really stiff. But as I need someone with me to get out and do physical things I can't at the moment find a solution. My PA and I have gone lawn bowling for the last couple of months once a week and have had a few short walks. I notice the difference when I have done this but I need more of that type of thing. Exercise makes my mood better as well as making my body feel better. As for 'enjoyment of sexual or sensual activities' I just know that this is never likely to happen. Because of my experiences I don't think I will ever have sex again. Even if I met someone I really liked I think the physical side of a relationship would just completely freak me out.

Another thing I had a lot to learn about was emotional internal and external resources. Internally I had to learn how to have a range of positive emotions. To be able to feel things like elation, joy and passion as well as the tender emotions like tenderness and contentment. To be able to do this meant I would not be taken over by and stuck within the negative emotions of anger and sadness. Externally, I had to learn how to express these positive emotions in my relationships either with people or animals. To have people with whom I could share these emotions with. I think that with Mary in particular I have had this ability for several years. Perhaps because she has also had mental health issues we understand each other and feel safe to share. With Joyce I could share a relationship which had feelings of tenderness, contentment and joy. Likewise, with Sara. It seems as though I can express a range of emotions within relationships that feel safe, trusting and caring.

When it comes to intellectual internal and external resources, the internal is still a problem. I tend not to be able to thinks things through or solve problems. My mind will instead go into a spiral of confusion. Thoughts rush around and I can't calmly think anything through. At the moment my external intellectual resources are quite limited because of the inner chaos. Learning things, reading, watching TV are all activities that I struggle with as my mind is full of memories of the past abuse.

A further avenue of internal/external resources which I am trying to pursue is that of art and creative pursuits. Internally this is the ability to express myself through such things as art, dance, writing etc. Externally it is having people to enjoy these creative activities with. I obviously have the ability to express myself through writing as I am writing this! I would like to regain my patience to paint. As previously mentioned this was something I was beginning to learn in Scotland but each time I try now it just ends in scribbles of frustration.

There are also material inner and external resources. Inner is the ability to earn a living, to enjoy material things etc. External is having a job, home and utilities. Since I was 30 I have only worked for three years apart from going to university in my 30s. Some people with DID are perfectly capable of holding down a good job but, unfortunately, I have never managed this since turning 30. I am not too bothered about material things except having the basics of life. This is probably because I still find it hard to buy things for myself. I don't feel that I deserve them. The only thing I am interested in is buying a new car every three or four years. But having a car is important, practically, and travelling by car is much safer than using public transport.

My spiritual inner and external resources seem to have died with Joyce. I was really interested in spiritual things. But with the passing of Joyce and my problems fighting those overwhelming emotions my spiritual side has been forgotten about.

The final internal and external resource is that of nature. Here, I did find the one resource I can totally relate to. By now I see nature as one of my biggest resources in the healing process. There is nothing that gives me more peace than nature. My biggest dream would be to win the lottery and buy a small cottage with a garden. I love seeing things grow and being aware of the seasons. I also love the beauty of sunrises and sunsets.

Looking at all these resources is interesting. If I have a bad day then it helps to sit and think what has happened that made it feel bad. Then to write down what my beliefs and judgements about myself are in my mind and how this shows itself in my body. Am I tense, how is my breathing, how is my posture? From there I can pick one of my resources. For example, looking at nature. If I concentrate of a sunset for example, how does this affect my mind and body? Doing a simple thing like this can have a huge effect on what I am thinking or feeling.

Chapter 14

Therapy Continues

I was still continuing to read through the chapters my therapist gave me, but not seeming to make much headway. I had been out of Respite for two weeks and felt I should still be there but would not admit to it. My PA and I started on an eight-week Mindfulness Course, and the second session caused huge problems. The trainer and about 15 of us were sitting in a circle and he suggested we shut our eyes and do a body scan exercise. Being in a circle of strangers and shutting my eyes was bad enough. Old fears were there. What were people doing? Was I in danger? Did I trust these people?

In the guided exercise we were to be aware of different parts of our body, starting at our feet. The aim was to sit with the sensation in each part of the body. Unfortunately, this led to me being flooded with memories and bodily sensations I could well do without. It got so bad that I left the room for the remainder of the exercise, trying to calm down and bring myself back into the present.

I needed to re-assess this so called 'recovery process' because it felt like I was getting worse instead of better. But I don't think I am abnormal in this. Others have felt the same way. I had to look at what was going on inside me. I decided it was actually getting worse because I was getting nearer to the trauma.

My defences had been dropping since I came to England and the emotions were rising to the surface. In Scotland Trish had been our protector, trying to ensure our safety from the memories and emotions. She still holds the barrier between Suzie and me, and the other four personalities who hold the most horrific memories. She helped us through university and mostly helped us to be emotionally safe from the emotional and physical pain. But pushing down the truth is not going to work forever. Yes, I did healing work in Scotland but because of the ongoing abuse Trish was still protecting, not allowing us to feel the emotions.

My therapist was giving me the chapters I have already mentioned. Plus, I had chapters on "grounding yourself", "Core Alignment: working with Posture" and "Using Your Breath". I will talk about these later; for the moment I need to discuss what was going wrong.

Just reading something does not work for me. Even when I can concentrate on all these concepts, they do not actually penetrate "my inner being". So just reading psychological theory is, for me, by and large a useless exercise. I need to be able to discuss what I have read. To try out the exercise with my therapist. To see what works for me and what does not. My other personalities need to be involved and to try out what works for them too. I think that after 20 sessions the only really useful thing I gained was sitting with my therapist imagining my "safe place". A place I could go to in my mind when the stress was getting too much. In a nutshell, my therapist and I were not singing off the same hymn sheet.

I can understand that she did not want to talk about memories with me because I am pretty unstable and struggling. Her view would be that if I talked about the memories I would become even worse. At least, I assume that this is what she was thinking. But I have these memories in my mind anyway, and the emotions are there. Getting me stable first just is not going to work because my emotions are unmanageable. So, half way through therapy I saw a huge problem on the horizon.

All these emotions are coming from the past and it is impossible to ignore them. I don't want to ignore them anyway because I believe that to recover and heal they need to be looked at and dealt with. It means that after a lifetime of denial I am emotionally waking up. This process started with Joyce's death, which pushed the emotional switch to the "on" position. Trish was deeply affected by her death and seemed to run out of the protective energy which had fuelled her for so long.

It's difficult to be faced with emotions after all these years

I think the only thing that all of my personalities have in common is fear. Fear of progress for some, fear of failure for others. It feels like an inner war and can certainly have an adverse effect on healing. So, for me, learning more about my parts is a necessity. Keeping a journal can work for this. We can all write what we feel or what we want. We can argue with each other through writing and sort out disagreements so that life can become calmer and make more sense.

My inner parts all have different needs and goals and will fight to get them met. One consequence of this is that we have difficulty with relationships. I have already mentioned the difficulty of keeping up with conversations because I "switch". On top of this is the fact that some us want a relationship and want to be loved but others would rather lock themselves away and never see anyone. I am not talking about sexual relationships, but any relationship.

There are many days I despair of ever recovering and thoughts of suicide are never too far away. But what is important is to look back and see how my personalities worked together to get us through the abuse. Dissociation truly is a gift as it got us through the unendurable. So, if all the parts of me helped me to survive them all the parts of me can help me to recover. Some parts of us do not like other parts of us. Some want to keep the emotions buried. Some hold memories that I don't know if they will ever share with me. They shared some of them with Janet but not me. Suzie finds it easy to trust Maike, Trish doesn't.

Many times, I have felt like I am having a nervous breakdown on the inside and trying to appear Ok on the surface. I think it is actually a sign that my mind is trying to heal. The longer I live in England, the louder my mind is crying out to heal. And I am discovering that this healing is a very personal thing. All people with DID are different so I don't think there is a "one size fits all" plan for recovery. A particular therapeutic approach may work for one person but not for another. What we do have in common is that recovery is a daily struggle.

There are aspects of recovery that all of us have to deal with. We have to learn to care for ourselves on a physical level and show ourselves compassion. These are things we did not experience or learn when we were young. In other words, we have to stop abusing ourselves. We have to commit ourselves to the belief that we can heal even when we don't feel it. And we have to develop a ton of patience.

So where does this leave me with the question of therapy. Carry on or give up? Without a doubt carry on. Therapists do not have the answers to give us, only we have the answers. I think part of the problem with my therapy is that the chapters she is giving me are not helping. While her motives are good her "chapter of the day" is not necessarily one that will help me on that day or the following week. I think it needs to be more collaborative effort. I am not a "child" waiting for the "adult" to tell me what to do. Therefore, I need to talk to her about having a joint plan. She has the professional knowledge that I do not, but it is my recovery and I need to be involved in planning our direction. I need to not feel disempowered in therapy as I have felt disempowered all my life. For my part, I need to be able to go to therapy with an open mind and try to communicate on a real level and not just on a superficial one.

Therapy though is not just the one hour a week session. That one hour is not going to bring recovery. I need to work at recovery between sessions putting into practice anything I have learned. If I make a new discovery about myself during a session I have to keep reinforcing it. For example, if I accept during a session that the abuse was not my fault I have to keep reminding myself of this over the course of the next days until it sinks in. I also have to find the stress busting things that work for me. Like nature, painting, meditating and grounding skills. Yes, that information is in the chapters I am given, but I need to discuss them more, finding out what works for me personally and what does not.

I know that I need to practice grounding skills. Because I dissociate a lot and am often in a state of hypervigilance I live too much in my head. Sara taught me a lot about body work. Being ungrounded leads me to feel off balance and unable to concentrate. It has been pointed out to me that my body is nearly always tense. I know that I tend to sit in a defensive way in an attempt to make myself feel safe from attack or to reduce my feelings of vulnerability. I do this even when there is no threat in reality. The result is tension in muscles or not even being aware of my body at all. Sara used to get me to stand with no shoes on, imagining a line from my head going down into the earth. Standing straight with relaxed arms and feeling the connection with the earth. This simple exercise felt good even though she said my posture was terrible. It still is terrible. I noticed recently in therapy when I was asked to sit up straight in my chair with hands on my thighs that I felt incredibility vulnerable and afraid. When I did Eurythmy in the Camphill Medical Practice I found those movements very grounding so it is important that I try to remember some of the exercises and begin to practice them again.

When I feel stressed it is interesting to note what feelings and thoughts I am having and then try a grounding exercise. Afterwards I try to write down the differences in my feelings, thoughts and body. The results are interesting but it takes time and practice. And the determination to do the exercise when I actually just find it easier to stay stressed.

How I hold my body gives out a message to other people. If my posture is anything to by, I am giving out messages of defensiveness or vulnerability. I think too that I try and hide my body. It is almost in the same way that a threatened animal protects its stomach, throat and genital area. I think I do the same. This hiding of my body is not just in posture but also in what I wear. I hate showing any flesh and therefore dress in jeans, high neck tops and long sleeves. Even going out without a jacket or a zip up hoodie is difficult. The fact that my cousin got me on the beach in a swimsuit was nothing short of a miracle. But some cousins you don't argue with! Actually, it felt like a major victory to me.

Chapter 15

Serious Surfacing of Memories.

In October of 2017 I started getting the feeling that a memory was about to about to surface. Certain words would begin to trigger me and I had no idea why. I felt there was a huge sense of fear coming from deep inside and could not figure it out. I tried to just live with the feeling and not push things. Part of me was afraid to know what this memory was anyway.

However, during a therapy session my therapist was showing me a diagram which basically just said 'abuser' and 'abused'. The memory just flew to the surface, and I went into shock. I remember stupidly asking the therapist why my jeans were shaking. I couldn't even figure out that it was me that was shaking and not my jeans. I stood up, leaned against the wall and went into a meltdown inside. Thankfully she had a free space immediately after so I stayed with her for over two hours, drinking coffee and popping outside for a smoke. Eventually I was in a state to drive home and Maike was coming that afternoon.

I guess it should have been obvious to me, that memory which one of my other personalities held, but it wasn't. Their memory was of the night before we moved in with Janet and Derek. I knew that I had been abused that night in a horrendous way, but the memories I held were nothing compared to the memory I got from Anne, one of my personalities.

I had believed up until that point that all the abuse had been done to me. But Anne's memory involved her abusing someone else

I just could not cope with this information and it threw my mind all over the place. How could a part of me have done that? How could I cope with that knowledge? How could I live with myself? How could I deserve a life? How could I expect the professionals around me to still care for me? How could I show my face in public knowing what that part of me had done? I was truly losing the plot big time.

My therapist tried to tell me that it was not my fault. That people in ritual abuse situations have no choice. They are forced into doing things. She said that she knew that I would never hurt anyone by choice. None of it got through to me. What I do remember though was her saying if I committed suicide my abusers would have won. However, I don't think I cared if they won or not.

The following week was a nightmare. Flashbacks of the event in great detail, nightmares, panic attacks, anxiety attacks and serious suicidal thoughts. I remember having phone calls with Maike. I don't remember much of what I said other than being hysterical lots of the time and her telling me to breathe. She asked if I wanted to go into respite but I held out for a week. At the end of that week I knew I couldn't do it on my own. I just didn't feel safe. So, I had a week in respite followed by a weekend with my cousin Lynn.

Lynn was aware of what the memory was as I had spoken on the phone with her. She was brilliant in her understanding and said that I could go to them rather than respite but I felt that I needed to be around professionals before I went to hers. At least in respite I felt safe from the prospect of killing myself and was getting the space to try and work things out a bit. When I went down to Lynn's for the weekend I was doing fine until she took me to her daughter's house and I had to meet up with other family members. I just did not want to be around people. On the way back, I fell out with Lynn, calling her a bitch for making me do it. She responded by saying that I had to face them sooner or later and it was best to be sooner. She too was of the opinion that the memory was not my fault.

Because of being in respite and at Lynn's I missed two therapy sessions. However, I was e-mailing Maike and being told by her to just take things one minute at a time. Even that seemed impossible sometimes. Lots of my time, before and after respite, was either spent in bed or under a fleece on the sofa being so terrified of myself that I couldn't stop shaking. I went out with my PA on the days that I had her but couldn't cope with people or the outside world.

On the third week I went to therapy. As I write this it was actually only last week. The therapist again told me it was not my fault. She said that what had happened to me made her upset and angry. Upset because of the things that had happened to me and angry that these things were still happening to others who had been in my position. She told me that even though the memory was of something that happened in 2001 it had only happened in my mind a month ago and it was going to take time to recover and come to terms with it.

Part of me wants to believe her, to believe that my support team still care and don't see me any differently. Part of me wants to believe that it was not my fault. But the other part of me still feels I am totally worthless, deserving of punishment and not care.

The feelings of shame, worthlessness and guilt were magnified. I think that people who have been abused often feel like this. I had spoken to Joyce years ago about these feelings but that was when I believed I had only been abused. At that time, I realised that I felt ashamed because I had been abused. I felt that

I was to blame for it because I was basically bad. I blamed myself for what the police did in Scotland. I blamed myself because I was not believed by the NHS in Scotland.

Now my suicidal thoughts were stemming from feelings of shame and being worthless. I did not think I deserved to live and be happy. Therefore, I thought that I should die. My hatred of myself was growing by the day. On top of the shame and guilt came intense fear. Fear of the parts of me that held the worst of the memories. Fear of what they were made to do. Fear of the hatred that people would feel towards me if they knew. A hatred that I actually feel would be more than justified.

I know that many people in ritual abuse settings have been made to do things they did not choose to do, but that does not make it any easier to deal with. I just felt disgusted with myself. Trying to see it logically was not helping. I know that in ritual abuse settings things are all about people having control over us, manipulating us into doing things. They use mind control as a form of torture to get people to do what they want. In reality I was powerless to fight them. I hate myself for being powerless and question 'was there anything I could have done to say no and walk away?'.

In reality there was nothing I could have done as their hold over me spanned over 40 years. With the coming of the memory I made the jump from hating my abusers to hating myself. But in truth I had always hated myself. The feeling just got magnified and all the hatred got directed inside.

These feeling of guilt and shame started to affect my relationship with my therapist and Maike. I felt vulnerable and needed support to get through this. But, on the other hand, I wanted to push them away. I felt unworthy of their care and support and guilty for needing help. I felt that they were being paid to say they cared so I couldn't trust what they said to me. I wanted to reject them before they rejected me.

My whole belief system went into overdrive when Maike cancelled an appointment at only an hours' notice. I had been sitting thinking about what I wanted to discuss with her when she rang and cancelled because she was needed in the office. Instead of accepting it at face value my brain went back into old patterns. Rather than seeing it for what it was my mind came up with every negative emotion I could think of. She didn't want to see me because she was disgusted with what Anne had done. She didn't care anymore. She couldn't cope with me. She knew I had been suicidal for weeks and wished I would commit suicide so she didn't have to put up with me anymore. All her words about us getting through this together, how she wasn't going anywhere, were just lies. I just wanted to tell her to F... off before she rejected me.

I had been sending her e-mails most days after the memory surfaced. It helped to keep me grounded but after she cancelled the appointment I stopped sending them. The trust had gone again, and I didn't believe she cared. I was in fact hurting myself more than her by staying silent. I rang the crisis team over the weekend more than I ever have but just ended up frustrated. Most of them said they did not understand DID so I could only talk about being stressed and suicidal and not why. Though they were all good and worked at calming me down I couldn't say what my real problem was. It just added to my feelings of shame. I was ashamed so I could not tell them the truth. I felt they would not cope if I did tell them. I felt that they would not believe that such things could happen. So, all the shame I felt throughout my life was still there. I was ashamed to be me.

Before the memory surfaced I was struggling with the fact that I could be a likeable person whom people genuinely wanted to help. But now all the old things I had been told all my life were painfully on the surface. I am bad, deserving of the abuse, useless and unlovable. Plus, there was the fact that I don't know who I am anymore. What other memories do my other personalities hold? When will the next memory come? How do I cope with having other personalities inside me that I hate?

I believe that the terrible memory truly caused a breakdown. All of my life I had managed to hold things together one way or another, but this was just too much. Having said that, maybe the breakdown was necessary. By holding things together, all I was really doing was surviving, not living. Perhaps I needed to break down in order to truly start the process of recovery. The past, however bad it may be needs to be faced and dealt with. My usual denial strategy is not going to bring about healing. From this point on my life is never going to be the same and I need to find ways to understand myself and deal with it all. I think my mind is telling me that after being in England for almost two and a half years it wants to heal.

Chapter 16

Moving Forward

So here I am today. Not 'recovered', exactly, but getting there. That's the thing I'm starting to learn. There's no such thing as 'recovery' as an end goal. What there is are healthy coping strategies, self-acceptance, coming to terms with your life as it is and working on ways to make it manageable.

My care package funding was given the ok. In July 2017 I was given funding to allow me to have 4 weeks of respite a year. Plus, I got a personal assistant for 8 hours a week. The funding for the PA was for 3 months. This is to help me to get out and attend groups. A support worker and I did the interviews and we decided on employing Helen for 4 hours twice a week. However, this changed quite quickly to a couple of hours 4 days a week. We started to go and play lawn bowls in an evening. I enjoy the bowls but struggle with the social side of it. I find it really stressful to be in a group of people and therefore will switch quickly between personalities. In practical terms, this means that I often hear the first part of a sentence but not the second. I become unaware of what I say. The more stressed I get, the worse it becomes. We tried going to an art course one afternoon and the same problem occurred there too. Too many people in close proximity.

We go shopping once a week for food. At least now I have food in the fridge but I still have a problem with eating it. One afternoon a week, we try cooking. Cooking works when I have someone with me. We are going to try a mindfulness course. Hopefully that will be easier as less conversation with strangers is needed. I like having Helen though because it is giving me more structure to my week. My cousins give me structure through my dog sitting and visiting them, but I need to build a life for myself.

I am learning to express and enjoy myself creatively – even in a playful way. Maike made a joke one day that she had to drive her car to come and visit me because her unicorn was ill! The picture of her on a unicorn was really funny. She suggested Suzie could draw her a picture of a unicorn. In turn Suzie left a note where I could see it saying "we have to draw Maike a unicorn". I drew the outline of the unicorn for her and she did basically the rest, colouring it in. It was the first time in two years that we had done anything artistic and it felt good. It did make me laugh though because I realised that Maike had suggested it to the right person. Anyone other than Suzie and it probably would not have happened. It was Suzie who put together the postcards and notelets that were sold at the Retreat Centre.

Although therapy is important and practicing new skills is important I need to have time for fun. Fun has not been a huge part of my life. Mary and I often had fun and I miss her not just for her company but for the fun we had. This Friday my PA and I are having a Fun Friday. Going to the coast, eating fish and chips and doing the charity shops.

The things I have discovered about myself in the last two years have been disconcerting to say the least. I realise that I have never truly lived. Yes, when I was with Janet and Derek I was functioning much better. In The retreat centre with Joyce I was learning a lot. With Sara I was learning too.

But in England I have discovered that I never did many 'normal' activities in my life. What I am attempting to do here are things that feel totally alien to me. Learning how to cope with emotions and learning how to be involved in social activities. That may not sound a lot when put in one short sentence. But in many ways in feels like having to rebuild myself. Maybe rebuilding is the wrong word. I am trying to be a me that I have never been before and, believe me, it is bloody exhausting. I am trying to cope with the past and come to terms with it. I am trying to do therapy and learn how my past affects the present. And trying to keep a sense of hope and belief that I can make myself a happy future.

At times, I feel as though I have walked into a brick wall and don't know how to keep going. My mantra though is that I am not a victim but a survivor and one way or another I will find my way through this.

There are things I need to focus on. The first of these is that I am not mad. Yes, I can behave in ways that may seem a little crazy to the outside world. Switching personality can look mad to others but it isn't.

The fact that I have DID gave me the capacity to survive the horrors of the abuse. I need to understand that my reactions towards people are based on my past experiences. If my home life in Scotland was not one of love and care, I could not develop a healthy sense of self. Neither could I develop healthy relationships with other people because I tend to see people as a threat to me.

I am not mad, but what happened to me was mad. It is mad that ritual groups can go to such lengths to destroy other people and get away with it. It is mad that society in general cannot begin to accept that these things happen.

It's also important to realise that I am not powerless anymore. I am in a safe environment now and can take back control of my own life. I need to concentrate on the fact that my healing is in my control. I can do it my way and in my time.

This does not mean starting from scratch though. It's important to remember the relationships I had in Scotland. The people who helped me there and began to teach me the things I have already discussed. I have knowledge that I can build on. I have experienced being cared for.

Now I need to look deeper inside myself and understand why my mind works in the way it does. This is not something I believe is possible on my own and I am lucky to have the professional support that I do. They can help me explore the things that I don't understand.

One thing I learned is that years of abuse left me feeling unprotected, rejected and overwhelmed with fear. This in turn meant I did not have the capacity to trust. I wanted to feel loved, cared for and protected but there was no-one who did. And I was so afraid of rejection that even if there had been someone I would not have known how to accept it. During the years of childhood, I developed the idea that I needed no-one because to do so was too frightening. But deep down somewhere I desperately wanted to be loved. With the friends I had in Scotland I could see that they cared but I was always waiting for the rejection. Joyce was the one person who taught me more about love than anyone. When thinking about how to get through this really stressful time my thoughts turn to her.

I believe that for me the way to healing is through love. To be able to have relationships where I do not fear rejection and where I can be totally honest. I also need to have a loving relationship with all the parts of myself. I also need to be honest with myself and stop denying my feelings and thoughts. I think initially this can only be done within the safety of my professional relationships. I need people who can hold the professional boundaries allowing me to feel safe from any more abuse. It's a bit like a child who needs to learn from within a safe base before they can move out to try things in the wider world. I have known Maike for over two years now and have done 48 sessions with my therapist. I know it's been hard for Maike when my trust comes and goes, and we can feel rejected at the drop of a pin. I think it's hard for my therapist who probably wonders what she has got herself into when I seem to just go from one crisis to another. But on the other hand, I am the one who is living with me 24 hours a day so I am finding it harder than they are.

With my emotions towards Maike and my therapist swinging from one extreme to the other it feels like we are all walking through a minefield. One minute I want them to care, the next I want to push them away. But at least I am beginning to understand why.

The biggest question I have to answer is 'who am I?'. At the end of the day I am the sum of all my parts so to get the answer I have to communicate with the other parts and get to know them. Vital in this process is to see myself as an individual and not as a Disorder. I am not a label. Originally my 'condition' was called Multiple Personality Disorder and then the name was changed to Dissociative Identity Disorder. But my personal opinion is that for me these labels just don't work. I would rather refer to myself as being Multiple. I have multiple parts which make up the whole. Therapists and psychiatrists refer to people like me as having a 'core' personality and several other 'alters'. I am not sure I agree with this. They would see me as the core personalities, but am I? My feeling is that I am no more important than my other parts. What I need is to have better communication between my parts so that we have more control over our lives.

Therapy with someone experienced in these matters is important, and the relationship I develop with the therapist is vital. It needs to be with someone who is consistent. Not someone who acts one way one week, and another the following week. We need to know where we are with a person. Abusers play love/hate games with our minds so consistency in our professional support system is really important. It also needs to be with someone who is caring and warm rather than aloof. A therapist and care manager who show compassion are good teachers. People like me find it hard to be compassionate towards ourselves. I can be compassionate towards others but not towards myself. If my therapist and care manager can stay consistent, compassionate, and honest with me then eventually I can perhaps learn that I am worthy of compassion. Then in turn I can learn to be compassionate with myself and my other parts.

To change therapists or care managers on a regular basis only leads to trauma and feeds into the past rejections. I also feel that a one-hour session a week is not enough. I recognise the time constraints within the NHS, but if all the parts of me need to talk to the therapist, that's going to take more than one hour a week. Perhaps it would be progress if the NHS allowed a longer session for people who are multiple. Not all of us are in the position of being able to pay for a private therapist, even if we found one experienced enough. One of the dangers within the NHS is the 40-session limit. Does the therapist rush things, thus leaving the patient alone at the end, in a more traumatised state?

Some therapists believe they should only talk to the person they see as the 'core' personality. For me this view is really damaging. Other parts of me are listening when I am at therapy and if they are ignored they feel rejected. If they feel rejected one or other of them will end up trying to sabotage the therapeutic relationship. I am more than capable of pulling back from my care manager and therapist if I feel criticised or rejected so it helps if my other parts are not getting offended too.

Criticism from my support team is another difficult area. I criticise myself all the time. I constantly feel I should be doing better, that my other parts are bad or worthless. In effect I am continuing the abuse that I suffered from others. I abuse myself by hating the parts I don't know. So, if any of my support team criticise me it feels like they are verbally abusing me.

Actually, I can see the funny side in what I have just written. People with DID must be a nightmare to treat. One week I want to see them and then they trigger something inside me and we want to tell them to go to hell. I am not saying therapists and care managers need to tip toe around me. My professionals certainly don't tip toe around me. We discuss things that are really painful and make me want to run a mile or ignore the conversation. But if we are all doing our best to work together we can sort out any problems as they arise. I think it is difficult and challenging for all of us. If anyone says that going to therapy is easy then I don't think they are really engaging with the process.

It's not just my professionals who need to make an effort. I need to as well. I need to be willing to be open, honest and vulnerable even when I want to fight them and withdraw. I need to put in the effort to try to understand the new concepts they tell me about. I need to be willing to work on my own between appointments. If I see them for an hour and then go home and continue living life using my old coping mechanisms I will not get anywhere. At the end of the day it is my recovery and it is my responsibility to keep working on whatever I have learned in a session.

A lot of people with DID know their other parts and can communicate with them. I can't. I know what kind of people Suzie and Trish are but we don't directly communicate with each other inside. As for the other four personalities I don't know much about them at all. Except for the memory that Anne shared. Sending e-mails to Maike is useful because often Trish and Suzie will write to her so I can learn what is on their minds. Sometimes we write to Maike too and I can read what they are saying. I think it is important, if my other parts talk in therapy, that my therapist tells me what has been said. It all helps me to get to know myself.

Sometimes at home Suzie will leave me notes. Usually notes to remember to buy her chocolate milk. Trish will leave notes reminding me of appointments. Sometimes I try to keep a daily journal of what time I have lost and sometimes Suzie or Trish will fill in what they have done in the gaps. But it feels like there is a long way to go. Trish and Suzie need to be more understanding of each other and learn to like each other more. We have a small Christmas tree that Joyce gave Suzie years ago. Suzie has been trying to put it out where she can see it but every time she does Trish puts it away again as she hates Christmas and wants nothing to with it. Years ago, I used to buy a small tree and decorate it only to discover that Trish had thrown it out. At least a little eight-inch one that Suzie has is still here years later. Not even Trish would throw out something that Joyce gave as a gift. Suzie loves going to my cousin Lynn's for Christmas as the house inside and out is like Santa's Grotto. Trish however hates the decorations and goes around wearing a Bah Humbug hat. So, there is a lot of work to be done to get those two more accepting of each other.

Healing and recovery is a long process but we need to remember that it is our process. It is not helpful to have a therapist who tells us how to heal. If we are told what we should do to aid our recovery we can feel as though our control is being taken away again. It's important that we are part of the discussions about any treatment/care plan. Everyone with DID is unique so there is not a 'one size fits all' cure. We are the experts in how our individual 'systems' work. We are the experts in how we see our recovery. We know if we want to integrate of if we want to live our lives being multiple. But we do need guidance.

I am lucky in having a team of support people and personally feel this is important. The things I am trying to recover from are immense and I don't think it would be possible with just one person. Apart from Maike and my therapist, there is a psychiatrist in the background. I can talk with the duty worker at the hospital where they are based. Out of office hours I have access to the crisis team and I have my PA for eight hours a week. There are times when I have difficulty with the crisis team. They are on the other end of a phone and very seldom do I get the same person twice. Though they have access to my care notes, very often they tell me that they do not understand DID. If I am in a crisis I need someone who understands and not someone who 'does not get it'. Yes, they can try to calm me down, but they don't understand the more complex issues. But having said that at least they are there and available in evenings and weekends.

Final Comments

This has very much been my own personal story and opinions. As I have said throughout, each person with DID is a unique person. The condition is the result of extreme trauma but this book is about my own experience of trauma. Others will have had different experiences.

We all have our own idea on what we see our healing process to be. Some want to integrate and some do not. Again, the fact that I want to live as someone who is multiple but with better 'internal' communication is my personal choice. It may turn out that years down the line I change my mind, or that integration may well happen. At this point the future is unknown.

Though there are differences between each person with DID. There are similarities. We have all suffered the experience of extreme trauma, perhaps over a period of a few years and perhaps over many more. I think that we all have experienced the difficulties of managing to get the correct diagnosis and correct treatment. Some of us are still struggling to get treatment of any kind.

We all struggle daily, not just with losing time but with the accompanying Complex Post Traumatic Stress that goes along with our DID. And we struggle with the physical issues we are left with as a result of prolonged abuse.

We have struggled with being prescribed medication which does not help our condition. Many of us have been diagnosed wrongly with Borderline Personality Disorder, for example, and given medication to deal with something that we do not have. There is no medication for DID, although sometimes medication can be helpful to ease the symptoms of Post-Traumatic Stress. Again, I believe that medicating us too much can be negative. It can leave us feeling numb. It's my personal view that to heal we have to face our fears and feelings and this will not be possible if we are numb.

There are things that are helpful for all of us. The things like learning skills to help us deal with our distress levels and flashback etc. I have mentioned these in different chapters.

If, as a survivor, you are reading this I would like to share just a few things that have become so important to me. The most important perhaps being that it has been my DID which has kept me sane. Without my other personalities helping me cope with the abuse I would probably be in locked ward somewhere or at the very least totally unable to function.

If you are free from the abusive situation, as I hope you are, then you now have control over your life. You can make your own decisions and choices. By making our own choices and decisions we can shape a life for ourselves.

No matter how bad your past abuse was you were not to blame for it. The blame lies firmly at the feet of those who abused you. You were controlled and manipulated and had no choice.

Recovery is hell, but it is possible. Keep believing in yourself because at the end of the day your recovery is in your own hands. You are no longer a victim. You are a survivor. People like us have an inner strength that we have to draw on every day. Some days we lack that strength, but that's ok. Take the time out that you need, knowing that you will keep trying.

I believe that the key to recovery is love. Learning how to accept love from others and learning how to love ourselves. Abuse has nothing to do with love and everything to do with control and hate. I am grateful that I have been on the receiving end of love. The people in Scotland who cared and loved for me during the years after 2001 know who they are and know how much I appreciate them. But the person I owe the most to is Joyce, who truly acted like a surrogate mother to me. She had faith in me when I didn't and she was the first person I truly trusted and loved in return. A few days before she died she asked me to finish this book as she thought it would help others. I hope it does help even a few people. So, what I have written is dedicated to her memory because if it wasn't for her I would not still be alive and able to tell my story.

Useful Contacts

- PODS: Positive Outcomes for Dissociative Survivors

  https://www.pods-online.org.uk/

- The Pottergate Centre for Trauma and Dissociation

  www.dissociation.co.uk

- International Society for Trauma and Dissociation

  www.isst-d.org

- Clinic for Dissociative Studies

  www.clinicds.co.uk

Useful Facebook Pages

- Pathway to Freedom. Dissociation DID Trauma & Abuse
- Ups & Downs in the UK & USA
- My Anxiety Companion
- Beating Trauma with Elizabeth Corey
- Trauma Dissociation
- Dissociative Identity Disorder Devon